GAME OF THRONES A-Z

GAME OF THRONES

MARTIN HOWDEN

AN UNOFFICIAL GUIDE TO ACCOMPANY
THE HIT TV SERIES

JOHN BLAKE

Published by John Blake Publishing Ltd,
3 Bramber Court, 2 Bramber Road,
London W14 9PB, England

www.johnblakepublishing.co.uk

www.facebook.com/Johnblakepub facebook

twitter.com/johnblakepub twitter

First published in paperback in 2012

ISBN: 978 1 85782 996 9

British Library Cataloguing-in-Publication Data:

A catalogue record for this book is available from the British Library.

Design by www.envydesign.co.uk

Printed and bound in Great Britain by CPI Group (UK) Ltd

3 5 7 9 10 8 6 4 2

© Text copyright Martin Howden 2012

Inside photographs © Getty Images

Papers used by John Blake Publishing are natural, recyclable products made
from wood grown in sustainable forests. The manufacturing processes
conform to the environmental regulations of the country of origin.

Every attempt has been made to contact the relevant copyright-holders,
but some were unobtainable. We would be grateful if the
appropriate people could contact us.

To Vanessa Danz, thanks for all your support and love while writing this book. Couldn't have done it without you, Fynn and Tallulah.

ADAPTATION

Fantasy series *A Song of Ice and Fire* had been declared by many – including, damningly, its own creator George R. R. Martin – unfilmable. It was too dense, filled with too many characters and had too many subplots to weave into a three-hour epic movie. The key word was 'too', and taking anything substantial out was like a house of cards: one misplaced stumble and it would all fall down.

You also have to factor in the fans. Devotion doesn't cover it, and cutting out swathes of text just to make a movie that captured the title and not the heart of the series would see a swift and sharp reaction. And, unusually for a fantasy series, these weren't your typical readers for this genre. Martin gave fantasy a mainstream jolt, thanks to pacey plotting, readable characters and intense action scenes. He gave his characters depth, eschewing the usual fantasy staples – hero, whore, villain and witch. They were real people in a real world – at least the one that Martin had created.

But there was another solution to solving the problem of 'too'. Adapting it for TV was always the obvious option. It allowed more breathing space but would still require patience. It wouldn't all be explained, and some plot lines would be frustrating to follow at first. However, there would be rewards, as Martin's world became clearer as the series went on.

Luckily, this wasn't a new thing for viewers of the small screen over the past couple of decades, and we have HBO to thank for this – the very company that would oversee the TV adaptation of the novels into *Game of Thrones*. HBO is unarguably the king of sophisticated viewing, thanks to its system of receiving money through subscriptions rather than advertising, which means it is not hampered by the usual restraints that hinder other network TV shows.

Following the success of shows like *The Wire*, *The Sopranos* and many others, viewers are accustomed to immersive worlds that take time to unfold their stories.

Characters are fleshed out rather than portrayed as having reached the pinnacle of human virtue. And unlike previous decades, when TV was seen as the ugly sister to cinema's handsome brother, the small screen can now be a byword for excellence, with many now preferring to while away their weekends with five- to six-hour bursts of a new world on TV box sets than going to the cinema.

A Game of Thrones' screen journey all began with a meal in 2006 between two young men and an older man, a portly looking wizard, usually dressed entirely in black. George R. R. Martin had heard it all before. These two young men weren't the first to come to him with a chance to tackle his mammoth series on the screen. Ever since the book was first published, he had been courted by Hollywood. And listen he would – ever polite, he would stifle his yawns and hold back on the eye rolling, as producers waxed lyrical about the franchise, while at the same time explaining all the scenes they would have to cut to make it into a movie. And then Martin would go home, declining the offer, despite, in his words, the 'truck loads of money' being offered. He had resigned himself to his series never being seen on the big screen.

But these two men that Martin continued to talk to long after lunch were convinced they could do the impossible.

Weiss remembers receiving a postal delivery of the books

and reading some of the pages. Some pages soon became hundreds, and it wasn't long before he was doing something he hadn't done since he was a child – devouring nothing but a book, and finishing it in a matter of days. He was hooked, as was Benioff.

Benioff told entertainment website *Collider*, 'When the books were originally sent to us, they were sent over to consider as feature adaptations. In reading them, the very first decision we made, probably a week after we started reading the books and having more fun than we have had reading anything in years, was that these were not going to work as features because there are such massive sprawling tapestries, so many characters and so many plotlines.'

The movie version, he explained, would have to simplify everything, and 'cut it down to maybe one storyline, so that it's the Jon Snow movie, or the Daenerys movie, or whatever else, and you are probably going to end up eliminating about 95 per cent of the characters, storylines and complexities. That wasn't interesting to us. We did want to adhere as closely as possible to George's world, knowing that there were going to be certain deviations, but we didn't want to get rid of so much of what made it special.'

Benioff also explained that, unlike many other fantasy series, these were books written for adults. 'This is not fantasy written for 12-year-old boys,' he said. 'Not to say that there aren't 12-year-old boys out there who would love it, but for the most part it's a more sophisticated readership, and we wanted to keep that. We wanted to keep the sexuality of the books. We wanted to keep the profanity. To have a PG-13 movie where Tyrion never gets to say the "C" word, it just wouldn't be Tyrion any more, and we wanted that. We wanted the brothel scenes. We wanted the bloody violence. You know that someone's head gets chopped off and you are going to see blood spurting out. You don't want to not do that because it's a PG-13 movie, and you only get two blood spurts per hour.'

Martin's meeting with Benioff and Weiss tickled him, and he came away thinking that maybe, just maybe, he had found his – admittedly small – band of warriors willing to risk it all to win their version of the Iron Throne – to adapt *A Song of Ice and Fire*.

Having flirted with the idea of a film, they too knew that it would have to be a TV series, and they pitched it to the only real network in town – HBO.

On 18 January 2007, Martin announced the news that fans of the book had been waiting for – HBO had optioned the series. 'Yes, it's true. Winter is coming to HBO,' he said, adding, '*A Song of Ice and Fire* should be in very good hands. I am thrilled to be in business with HBO.'

However, Martin, a veteran of TV, was quick to warn excited fans that a 'long and winding road awaited'. He added, 'A television series does not spring up full-blown overnight, of course. You won't be watching *Game of Thrones* on HBO next week, or telling TiVo to record it next month. Maybe this time next year you'll be seeing Tyrion and Dany and Jon Snow in those HBO promo spots.

'HBO liked it, I've been told, and they're doing a budget on it now, but they still haven't given it a green light. Of course, the writers' strike has hit now, so there's no telling what's happening in Hollywood. But HBO is what I've wanted for this from the beginning. The book series will be about 10,000 manuscript pages when it's all done, so the story's just too big for even a series of movies. And there's a lot of sex and violence, which is one reason I couldn't look too seriously at the broadcast networks. HBO can do it the way it would have to be done. I've got my fingers crossed. It's all in HBO's hands now.'

He should have heeded the warning himself. Unfortunately, it wouldn't be a year later at all – and, indeed, a frustrated Martin told his fans via a blog post in June 2008, '*A Game of Thrones* remains a script in development, not a series in production.'

In another blog post, he added, 'From the start of this, I've told myself, "Don't get too emotionally invested in this, or you will be devastated if it doesn't go." Wise words, those. I'm a smart guy. But easier said than done. I've failed. I am totally emotionally invested, and if HBO does indeed decide to pass, for whatever reason, I will be gutted. So let's all hope I am soon doing the happy dance instead.'

Originally, 12 hours were expected for each series, which was then pushed down to 10. David Benioff – who described the series as *The Sopranos* in Middle Earth – and D. B. Weiss had a plan for them to adapt a novel per series and for the two of them to write all the episodes bar one each season – with Martin tasked with the remaining one. However, that wouldn't be the case, and other writers joined the team.

While Martin would write an episode per season, he didn't spend much time on set. Calling a writer on to the film set, he said, is as 'useful as nipples on a breastplate'.

The first season finally premiered on 17 April 2011, marking both the end, and indeed the start, of years' worth of sweat and tears. Benioff admitted that it was a 'scary process' working on the show, forging ahead with a wildly ambitious project, while trying to ignore the insistent nagging in his head that there might not be an audience, knowing that all this work can be for nothing when adapting a hit book doesn't translate into viewing figures.

Martin was nervous as well, telling the *Guardian*, 'They did great stuff with historical drama in *Rome*, the western in *Deadwood*, the gangster thing in *The Sopranos*. They've redefined each of these genres, took it to a new level. So they thought, "We could do that in fantasy, too." Right now, it's more excitement I'm feeling, but I do have moments of, "Oh God, what if it's terrible, if it's a flop?" I worked out of Hollywood for 10 years – on shows including *The Twilight Zone*, as well as a handful of pilots that never saw the light of day, and I had my heart broken half a dozen times, so I know all the things that can go wrong.'

Luckily, that wasn't to be the case, and Weiss and Benioff breathed a sigh of relief when the first two seasons proved there was an audience for mainstream fantasy.

Martin himself has said about the adaptation of his series, 'I like the fact that David and Dan are doing a faithful adaptation, so, when the scenes are the scenes from the books, I like those. And I like almost all of the new scenes, not from the books, that David and Dan and the other writers have added.'

But he admitted he missed the scenes that are left out, 'the scenes from the books that are not included in the TV show that I wish they would have included. As I watch a show I'm always thinking, "Oh, this is coming next," and then that scene isn't there. But I understand the necessity for that. We have 10 hours and that's all we have. You cannot put every line of dialogue, every incident, in the TV show. You have to cut to the chase. I do rather wish we had more than 10 hours. Not a lot more: 12 hours per season would be ideal … If we had had those extra two hours, we could have included some of those small character scenes that would have helped develop the characters more and flesh them out; develop their depth and contradiction and be a little subtler. But we don't have 12 hours; we have 10. And, given that, I think the television show is extraordinary.'

ARYA STARK

The second daughter of Eddard and Catelyn Stark, nine-year-old Arya is a tomboy. Singing songs about queens and worrying about who she will marry isn't something that Arya does. She likes to play with the boys, learn about dragons and sword fight. Realising this, her half-brother, Jon Snow, gives her her first sword, which she calls Needle.

She is taken, along with her father and sister, Sansa, to King's Landing, and it soon becomes clear their lives are in danger. Realising he can't quell his feisty youngster, her dad finds a sword instructor for her. She loves her lessons with the eccentric Syrio Forel. He teaches her in the flamboyant Braavosi style but ends up defending her for real following the death of her father.

Arya manages to escape from the castle and lives off the street looking for food. She is found in the crowd during the execution of her father by Yoren, a member of the Night's

Watch. He forces her to look away when her dad is beheaded, and then chops off her hair so she can pass as a boy.

They are eventually captured, and taken to Harrenhal and made servants. During her journey there, Arya rescues a man named Jaqen, who tells her he will kill three people for his life and the two other lives that she saved. At this point, she had already created a hit list of people that had wronged her. Arya eventually escapes Harrenhal, and finds out that Jaqen can change his face. He gives her an iron coin in case she ever needs him again.

SPOILER

During her journey, Arya is discovered by the Brotherhood Without Banners, but she ends up being captured by The Hound later. His plan is to reunite her with her brother Robb in turn for a reward. However, they end up at the location where the events of the tragic Red Wedding take place. As her brother and men are being slaughtered, The Hound has to knock Arya out to ensure her safety. He takes her to the Vale of Arryn, which is ruled by her aunt Lysa.

She eventually heads to Braavos to use her coin, and is initiated into the guild of the Faceless Men – the shadowy group of assassins that Jaqen was a member of.

Following her training, Arya drinks some milk, which blinds her the next morning. Taking on the guise of a street urchin, she becomes better at lying and detecting the lies of others. She regains her sight after passing a test.

After she kills her first target, Arya is told she will begin her proper apprenticeship.

Arya is played by Maisie Williams. She had grown up loving drama but always thought of herself as a dancer. When she was 10, she enrolled at Susan Hill's School of Dance. Williams said about her time there, 'After I had been there a while, Sue suggested I attend a talent show in Paris. I came away from this with an agent and an audition with Pippa Hall, a children's casting director, for *Nanny McPhee 2*.'

During the audition process, Williams met Eros Vlahos (who plays Lommy Greenhands). 'I didn't get the part but did get down to the final two,' she said. 'At the time I was really disappointed, but I now realise that I did well to get that far. My agent, Louise Johnston, then put me up for an audition for Arya. I have to say that at first I wasn't too keen, I was still thinking about *Nanny McPhee 2*. But all auditions are good experience, so I went along and after the first audition in London I knew I wanted to be Arya!'

She was to have three auditions in total for the part. 'The first audition was in London at the end of June; it was very quick, recorded on video with lots of others all auditioning for Arya, Sansa or Bran. I was thrilled when after a few days I got a call back. The second audition was much longer; I had to do the same scene (a Kingsroad scene not used in the actual series) about five times with three different girls auditioning for Sansa, one of whom was Sophie Turner. We immediately got on well and both wanted each other, and ourselves, to get the parts so that we could meet again. I also did an Arya and Gendry scene from book two. The final audition was a screen test with David Benioff and Nina Gold at the beginning of August. I really enjoyed it and I thought it went quite well.

'We were packing up to go home from [a family] holiday in Scotland a few days after the final screen test when Louise, my agent, called and asked to speak to me. I knew there was good news when Louise asked to speak to me before she spoke to my mum; bad news comes from Mum, good news from Louise. I was so excited, I couldn't believe it. Then a few days later we found out that Sophie was playing Sansa. I WAS SO EXCITED! It was a dream come true! It took a while to sink in but it was the best thing ever!'

A SONG OF ICE AND FIRE

A Song of Ice and Fire is, according to the book series' author, George R. R. Martin, his 'magnum opus'. 'It's the biggest thing I have ever done and it's the most ambitious book I have ever done,' he said.

He began the series in 1991, while he was writing another book. While writing, an image of things called 'direwolves' suddenly blazed in his mind, and that image would quickly spread itself – until in no time at all he would have the first chapter in his head.

'Then I wrote the second chapter, the third chapter and suddenly I knew I was deep into this,' Martin said. 'At first I was thinking, "Is this a short story" or "Is it a novella?" "No, it's going to be a book; it's going to be a trilogy."'

In 1991, he had already settled on the book being a trilogy. 'Trilogies in fantasy have been very much in style since Tolkien, Martin explained. 'But then Hollywood stuff came up, and I put it in the drawer for a couple of years while I did pilots and so forth. When I picked it up in '94, I sold it as a trilogy. But then, over the course of finishing that first book, it rapidly became apparent that I wasn't going to get to the place that I wanted to by the end of all these thousands of pages.

'So then I started talking about four books, and by a certain point in the process I started talking six books. I skipped right over five – I never ever thought it would be five. I don't write things in blood, but seven feels right. Seven gods, seven kingdoms, seven books – there is a certain elegance to that that I would like to retain. That being said, the main thing is to tell the story – not to rush the story or to squeeze things.'

Part of the appeal is that each chapter takes on the perspective of another point of view, thus changing the characters from hero to villain and vice versa, as we hear people's inner thoughts. 'We all have reasons for the things we do, even the things that might look evil from the outside,' explained Martin. 'Sometimes they're based on mistaken assumptions or innate selfishness or psychological compulsions, but they're still reasons. Some of my science-fiction stories dealt with this theme of telepathy. If we could read other's minds, would that lead to universal love and understanding or would it lead to universal revulsion?'

The first book in the series received a positive reception, with critics praising *A Game of Thrones* for being more than just a sword and sorcery epic. It won several awards, including the Locus Award in 1997. *Clash of the Kings* was released in 1998, also winning the prestigious science-fiction Locus Award, and was also praised by critics.

The third book, *A Storm of Swords*, was released in 2000, with a novella entitled *Path of the Dragon* – a compilation of some of the chapters about Daenerys Targaryen – preceding it. For series three of the show, the producers went against their original manifesto of one series per book, and split the mammoth book into two series. Some countries split the paperback edition into two parts – *Steel and Snow* as part one, with part two entitled *Blood and Gold*. And in France they went as far as splitting it into four editions.

A Storm of Swords was nominated for the hugely prestigious Hugo Award, but lost out to J. K. Rowling's *Harry Potter and the Goblet of Fire*. The story continues the saga of the Five Kings and Daenerys' return to Pentos with her plans to invade the Seven Kingdoms. The novel features one of the most talked-about scenes in the series – the Red Wedding – which is looked at in greater detail later on in this book. *A Storm of Swords* debuted at number 12 in *The New York Times* bestseller list.

Martin's idea was that his next book would be shorter and more like his previous book *A Clash of Kings*. *A Dance with Dragons* was originally set five years after *A Storm of Swords*, but he realised the five-year plan didn't work for certain characters, and so *A Feast for Crows* became the fourth book, picking up after *A Storm of Swords*, with Martin scrapping the five-year gap.

The story was organic and proving hard to tame. Soon, the book was longer than *A Storm of Swords* – and he hadn't even finished it. Martin was reluctant to cut parts of the story and cut down on the characters. The publishers wanted to split the book into *A Feast for Crows*, parts one and two, but Martin was reluctant to go with that option, and felt the first part didn't have the sort of resolution to his characters that his fans were familiar with.

However, a friend of his suggested that, instead of splitting the story into two parts, he divide it geographically into two parts – the first part being *A Feast for Crows*, the other *A Dance with Dragons*. It meant he could postpone the unfinished character arcs and move them into the later book.

Martin has said about the split, 'I regret the necessity to split the books, but if I had to split them, then I think geography is preferable to chronology for a variety of reasons.' It was released in 2005, heading straight to the top of the bestseller lists, and saw Martin being dubbed the 'American Tolkien'.

Unsurprisingly, the story split meant the fates of some characters were left unresolved, but the author had stated the fifth book would be released the following year. However, the dates were constantly pushed back, and it would, in fact, be six years before *A Dance with Dragons* was published. In the meantime, the book was sold to HBO, and years of development saw a script finally being made, a pilot ordered and a series subsequently shown.

The last two books promise to be just as long, if not even longer. The penultimate instalment will be called *The Winds of Winter*. The seventh book will be entitled *A Dream of Spring*. It's believed the book will be the final one, but

Martin has said he is only firm about the ending of the series 'until I decide not to be firm'.

While he writes with the major plot points in mind, he is a writer who lets his story unfold as he goes along. He told *Rolling Stone* magazine, 'I have names for these types of writers – I call them architects and gardeners. The architect, before he drives a nail into a plank, has all the blueprints and knows what the house is going to be like and where the pipes are going to run. Then there are the gardeners, who dig a hole in the ground and plant a seed and water it – with their blood sometimes – and something comes up. They know what they planted, but there's still a lot of surprises.'

He went on, 'Now, you seldom get a writer who is purely an architect or purely a gardener, but I am much closer to a gardener. I know the ultimate end of the series and I know the fates of all the principal characters, but there's a lot of minor characters and details that I find along the way. For me, both as a reader and a writer, it's about the journey, not the ultimate destination.'

Martin explained he liked to use the metaphor of a journey. 'If I set out from New York to Los Angeles, I can look at a map and know that I'm gonna go through Chicago and then Denver. But that doesn't mean I know what's around every turn and bend of the journey, where there's gonna be a detour or there's gonna be a hitchhiker.

Those are the things I discover on the journey. And that, for me, is the joy of writing.'

Martin has told Benioff and Weiss the main plot points in case anything happens to him, but he will not permit another writer to finish his novel.

'Well, there's an element of my fans who are constantly pointing out my mortality to me and writing me letters about what plans I have made for when I die, and who's going to finish the series. I'm not planning on dying soon. I have a few health problems that come with age, but I'm in pretty good health. I hope to have another 20 years or so – plenty of time to write and who knows how medicine will have advanced by then? Maybe I'll be immortal. I would like that.'

He didn't help tone down fans' expectations when, after finishing the previous book, *A Feast for Crows*, it was suggested that work had already finished on *A Dance with Dragons* in 2005. 'This is a common misconception,' he told *Entertainment Weekly*. 'Parts of *A Dance with Dragons* were finished in 2005, when I finished *A Feast for Crows*. It's not like I had two complete books. I had one complete book, and one that was partially written. And I made an estimate as to how long it was going to take me to translate that partial book into a full one, and it was a woefully optimistic guess. What can I say? It's taken a lot longer.'

There are fears that the TV show will eventually be ahead

of the book – not something that worries Martin. He told *Rolling Stone* magazine in 2012, 'I have a considerable head start. But check with me in another year – I might have a different answer! I have a number of other projects that I'm juggling; I have to clear the decks so I can concentrate on the books. I have to learn to say no when people approach me for a short story or foreword. Last week, I spent the entire week writing introductions, for three different books. The truth is I'm a slow writer, no matter what I do, whether it's a giant fantasy epic or a foreword. "This is only a thousand words; you can knock it off in an afternoon." No, I can't, I'll be sweating over it for three days.'

He added in another interview, 'It has been a long journey. I think I'm starting to see it, but that's still a very long tunnel. The last book was 1,500 pages in manuscript. I think each of the next two will be at least as long, so that's 3,000 more pages that I still have to write, and that's a considerable amount of writing. I write one chapter at a time, one scene at a time, one sentence at a time, and don't worry about the rest. Step-by-step, sooner or later, the journey will get me there.'

Another time, he joked, 'Two BIG books. 1,500 manuscript pages each – that's 3,000 pages. I think I have a good shot. And you know, if I really get pressed, I've already established that red comet. I can just have it hit Westeros and wipe out all life!'

While some fans are impatient, Martin has his bone of literary contention – namely that genre authors still don't get the credit they deserve. 'I wouldn't use the phrase "literary highbrows", which is sort of reverse-elitist,' he says. 'But I do think fantasy and science fiction are a legitimate part of literature. I think I speak for virtually all fantasy and science-fiction writers that it's a constant annoyance for anyone who works in these fields that, whenever a great piece of work is produced, you get reviewers saying, "Oh, this isn't science fiction, it's too good." Most recently, that's happened with Cormac McCarthy and *The Road*. Which is definitely a science-fiction book, and yet it's winning all these prizes and people are saying, "No, no, it's science fiction." Well, it's literature *and* it's science fiction. It's a breath mint and a candy mint!'

After Martin finally finishes his epic series, he has detailed his plans for the future: 'I might write a science-fiction novel as my next major project after I finish *Ice and Fire*. I never left horror; I'm not going to leave fantasy. I try to do everything. I enjoy murder mysteries – maybe I'll write a murder mystery next. I just don't want to be told, "Oh, you write this sort of thing, so please settle down and keep turning out the same thing for ever." That would be boring.'

AWARDS

Befitting a show that has been lauded by critics and fans, *Game of Thrones* has been handsomely rewarded with prestigious prizes. It has been honoured numerous times. Here are the notable prize-giving entries for 2011 and 2012:

- It won the AFI TV Award for Program of the Year in the USA.
- Nina Gold was nominated for Outstanding Achievement in Casting in the Artios Awards and Outstanding Casting for a Drama Series at the Emmy Awards.
- The series was nominated several times at the 2011 Emmy ceremony, including a directing nod for Tim Van Patten and a win for Peter Dinklage in the Outstanding Supporting Actor in a Drama Series category.
- Dinklage also won the Best Supporting Actor – Series, Miniseries or Television Film at the Golden Globes. He was also honoured at the Satellite Awards and Scream Awards in 2011.
- Sean Bean and Lena Headey were also nominated at the Scream Awards – with *Game of Thrones* winning Best TV Show.
- Best TV Show at the *Kerrang!* Awards in 2012, and Program of the Year at the Television Critics Association Awards, with Peter Dinklage nominated.

- The series received many nominations at the 2012 Emmy Awards, including Outstanding Drama Series, Outstanding Casting for a Drama Series, Outstanding Costumes for a Series, Outstanding Prosthetic Makeup for a Series, Outstanding Special Visual Effects and Outstanding Supporting Actor in a Drama Series (Peter Dinklage)

B

BRANDON STARK

Brandon, or Bran as he's also known, is a young boy and the second son of Eddard and Catelyn Stark. He is a keen climber and can regularly be seen scaling the walls of Winterfell. However, he ends up in the wrong place at the wrong time, spotting the visiting Queen Cersei and her brother Jaime having sex. When he is discovered, Jaime pushes him from the window.

He survives, but is in a coma. Unbeknown to him, his direwolf thwarts an assassination attempt on his life while he is bedridden. While in the coma, Bran has visions featuring a three-eyed crow.

When he wakes up from the coma, he discovers he is a cripple, but is given the chance to continue riding thanks to a contraption devised by Tyrion Lannister. During one of his rides, he is ambushed by a group of wildings. They are all killed by Robb and Theon, bar a woman called Osha. She is taken back to Winterfell as prisoner, but eventually Osha bonds with Bran over his dream. He realises that he can see through the eyes of his direwolf.

SPOILER

When they flee Winterfell following Theon's betrayal, they eventually end up in the Haunted Forest in search of the three-eyed crow. He meets the Children of the Forest, and Bran learns about his gift. He can see things from the past by looking through the weirwoods, but his gift has yet to be fully realised.

Bran Stark is played by Isaac Hempstead-Wright, a young 13-year-old actor hailing from England. His other screen credit is playing Tom in the 2011 British horror *The Awakening*.

He says about being cast in the role, 'It was just an accident really. I go to a small acting group, and I heard *Game of Thrones* were doing a huge casting and so I went to the audition. I hadn't done an audition like this before.'

He watches it with his family, but admits there are some scenes that leave him a bit embarrassed to watch.

CASTING

In May 2009, Peter Dinklage signed on to star as Tyrion Lannister. Author George R. R. Martin and co-creator of the series David Benioff wanted Dinklage, and also Sean Bean, early on. 'Peter and Sean were the exceptions to the long, drawn-out casting process because we knew we wanted them from the beginning,' he said, 'so, we obviously didn't ask either of them to audition.'

It was then a case of going after the two actors. 'I had met Peter before, socially. We have a mutual friend, so I got his email address and sent him an email that just said, "I don't know if you have heard of these books, but there is a character named Tyrion Lannister and I think you would be fantastic. Maybe we could talk about it at some point." So, we started emailing, and then he came out to LA. We sat down with him and had a great conversation, where he basically said, "I am really interested in this part, but don't give me a beard. Dwarves in fantasy movies always have big beards. It's the cliché of fantasy." So, we promised him that he wouldn't have to have a beard, and that went well.'

And with Bean it was even easier. 'I had actually worked with Sean before and was just a huge admirer of him, as a professional and as a person. We had lunch with him in London and talked to him about the part, and we managed to get him.

'With Peter and with Sean, we just knew from midway through reading the first book that those were the actors we wanted.'

In July, more names were cast. Kit Harington landed the role of Jon Snow; Jack Gleeson won the part of Joffrey Baratheon; and Mark Addy was cast as King Robert Baratheon.

August saw Jennifer Ehle confirmed as Catelyn Stark, with Nikolaj Coster-Waldau, Tamzin Merchant, Richard Madden, Iain Glen, Sophie Turner, Maisie Williams and Alfie Allen all heading to the magical world of Westeros. Lena Headey joined the cast in September and Jason Momoa was hired for the part of Khal Drogo in October.

Michelle Fairley would replace Ehle as Catelyn after the pilot had been shot, with Emilia Clarke replacing Tamzin Merchant as Daenerys Targaryen.

Author Martin played an integral part in the casting process. While he wouldn't be present, the screen tests would be filmed and he eagerly viewed them every morning in the hope he could find the right person. Despite having an involvement, he knew the final decision rested with Weiss and Benioff.

With casting announced, Martin faced a problem common to writers who have their work adapted to the screen. Would his style change because he now knew what the characters looked like in the flesh? 'It does affect me when watching adaptations of other books by other writers,' he told *Empire*. 'For example, I recently read *The Hunger Games* and saw the movie, and I think if I go back and read that book now I will see those actors; but it doesn't happen with my own work. I've been living with these characters since 1991 in some cases; their images are fixed very strongly in my head, and it would be very difficult to replace them with our actors, good as they are. Also, I've seen dozens of other versions of these characters in the comic books, the card game, the book covers. These are characters that change over and over again, so there are a wealth of characterisations to choose from.'

Benioff said of the casting decisions in season two, 'You

decide if you absolutely need somebody who is well known to play a role. And you have that cost-cutting analysis. I sound like an accountant but, honestly, it's something we never came up against this year. It wasn't like we said, "We need Daniel Day-Lewis to play Stannis." [The new actors'] performances were so compelling and so overpowering that we decided that this person is far and away the most interesting person we saw for this role. Like Gemma Whelan came in for the role [of Theon's sister] and I seem to remember her not looking the same as the character in the book. But she is the character now and so overpoweringly great that I can't imagine anybody else being the character.'

For series three, Dame Diana Rigg will play Olenna Tyrell, the Queen of Thorns. Of the part, she said, 'I am thrilled, it's an absolutely wonderful part.' While *Office* star Mackenzie Crook will play wilding raider Orell. Crook said, 'It's a monster of a show, but it's a real privilege to be a part of this massive cast.'

Other key and new cast members include *Waking the Dead*'s Tara Fitzgerald as Stannis' wife, Selyse Florent, Clive Russell as Brynden The Blackfish Tully, who promised fans that the show will be as 'sexy, spectacular and violent as it has been up till now', and Nathalie Emmanuel will play slave-trader translator Missandei.

Tobias Menzies stars as Catelyn Stark's younger brother

Edmure Tully. The role of Qyburn will be played by Anton Lesser. Paul Kaye will star as Thoros of Myr, a member of the outlaw band the Brotherhood Without Banners; *Love Actually* star Thomas Brodie-Sangster will play Jojen Reed, a mysterious young man who aids Bran Stark; and Richard Dormer portrays Beric Dondarrion, the Brotherhood Without Banners leader. The eldest daughter of Howland Reed, Meera, a fervent Stark loyalist, will be played by Ellie Kendrick. Kristofer Hivju is playing Tormund Giantsbane, while Philip McGinley will be seen as Anguy, a key member of the Brotherhood Without Banners. Finally, *Misfits* star Iwan Rheon has landed a major part in the series, believed to be Ramsay Snow – the bastard of Roose Bolton.

It was announced in May 2012 that the character Mance Rayder would feature in season three, too. He had been mentioned several times during the series, but *Entertainment Weekly* confirmed he would finally appear on screen. As the King-Beyond-the-Wall, Rayder is a fan favourite, and there had been much talk about who would play the character, with a host of names including *Lost*'s Henry Ian Cusick, *Star Trek*'s Karl Urban and *Casino Royale*'s Mads Mikkelsen.

James Purefoy, however, remained the favourite for the role of Rayder, with the actor having expressed an interest in appearing on the show, saying, 'If it was the right role on *Game of Thrones*, definitely. Of course! It's a terrific series.

It's a great series of books. I love HBO. I'm on record saying that HBO is the best television company in the world, and I believe they are. I think they absolutely understand how to make television that is really, really vital and interesting and visceral, and all the things that television really should be.'

The Wire star Dominic West revealed in August 2012 that he turned down a major role in *Game of Thrones* because it would have involved being 'in Reykjavik for six months' – with many believing it was that of Mance. He told the *Huffington Post*, 'I was offered something on *Game of Thrones* and unfortunately I hadn't seen it, but my nephew and his father said, "Gosh, *Game of Thrones* is the only great show on!" And I felt terrible because I'd just turned them down; it was a lovely part, a good part. I'm going to regret it. My problem is, I've got four kids and, at the moment, I'm reluctant to be away from home for a long time. I can get a lot of work in London and still be at home.'

The actor who would play the part of Mance Rayder was finally announced on 17 August, and it was *Rome* star Ciaran Hinds who had won the role.

COSTUMES

Typifying the genre-breaking tradition of the show, when costume designer Michele Clapton was asked to submit one episode of the series for a chance to be nominated for a prestigious Emmy, she surprised many by opting out of the expected path of showing the glamorous gowns that Lena Headey wears as Cersei, or the Alexander McQueen-inspired tunnel dress for Margaery. Nor did she want to showcase the lavish and outrageous designs that adorn the gluttonous trading city of Qarth, for example. Instead, she went for a less obvious approach, choosing the gritty locales and grubby clothing of series two episode 'The Prince of Winterfell'.

'There's a big hole that fantasy often falls in,' she said. 'The costumes don't resonate with the environment. We try to give the costumes a reality based on the land, climate and the food sources. I want you to be able to smell the costumes.'

Clapton prepares extensively for each season, eventually meeting up with her assistant designers about four months before shooting to decide on the direction for the forthcoming episodes, what new characters need to be included and what influences suit different groups. Medieval England was an obvious choice for the North, but others include the Bedouins look for Dothraki and Inuit tribes for the people Beyond the Wall.

Clapton told the *LA Times*, 'It's so exciting because we can almost go anywhere as long as it makes sense. If they live on a windy, rocky island, like the Greyjoys do, then they dress accordingly. They have costumes made of heavy, densely woven cloths that are waxed and painted with fish oil to help keep out the wind. Everything has a reason for being there.

'We made all the costumes for the North from skins. For research, we looked at the Inuits and at Tibetan tribes – we try and look at peoples in different times in history to see how they would have dressed in that environment.

'I also looked at Lascaux cave paintings in France; they have these wonderful animal paintings. We decided that every time they killed an animal, the hunters would have to paint an animal onto their costume. The better the hunter, the more covered in these drawings he would be, which I think visually is really strong. We're always looking for ways to show who the leader is.'

Clapton is also allowed freedom to deviate from the book if needed, citing the example of King Renly, whose posse of rainbow warriors was excised from the screen as Clapton didn't think it would translate from the book.

Instead, she is allowed to use her own and her team's imagination. 'From these discussions we will create mood boards for each new place, and I will start to draw for principals. We will also travel to Italy, Paris and Madrid to look at fabrics, as well as scout London – mainly Shepherds Bush, Chelsea Harbour and Berwick Street.'

After weeks of research, she locates to the workrooms,

home to her cutters, markers and armourers. She prefers to make as much of the clothing and items in-house as possible because it is 'practical and much more fulfilling'.

'We have weavers, embroiderers and printers, so a lot of costumes are created from scratch,' Clapton added. 'Craster's wives' costumes, for instance, were woven from raffia, rabbit skin and feathers, which were then aged in our breakdown rooms. Likewise, Daenerys Dothraki's costume was woven in-house. Each season we try to hire less costumes, although we sometimes have to commission some extras' costumes to be made outside of the work-room due to time and numbers, but we still try to finish them on site.'

From there, it's on to filming. Despite the hard work that's gone into creating these costumes, many of them blend into the background, perversely hidden from your eyes, despite the blood and tears of craftwork that has gone into them. Filming also possesses a whole new host of challenges for Clapton. 'One big thing is: the children keep growing! I mean, in all ways: outwards and upwards! But that aside, sometimes you don't get to see the actor until quite close to shooting and, at that point, we are already quite a long way with the armour. With Brienne, for instance, she is a woman but we want to mistake her for a man; however, no matter what you do, women have hips. We just started making the lines on the armour go away from her waist and slowly she began to look more masculine; at the same time, the armour also had to be functional.'

As well as the costumes, the show's hair designer, Kevin Alexander, inspired some of the other big visual talking points in the series.

Around 30 wigs are used in the show, with Emilia Clarke, Lena Headey, Carice van Houten and Natalie Dormer all wearing hairpieces that cost around $7,000 each, with hair sourced from India and Russia. Because of the hefty price tags, the wigs are washed, styled and indulged in glamorous products every few days.

Sophie Turner, who plays Sansa, has blonde hair in real life, but because she was only a teenager it was decided that they didn't want to use peroxide on her – preferring instead to use around four different watercolour shades – which last around 10 days and need to be touched up constantly.

Jack Gleeson, who has naturally dark hair, needs his hair touched up daily, as well as kept short, as it makes him look younger for the role of evil young king Joffrey, who has blond Lannister locks.

Not everything is so glamorous and styled, however – multiple product brands, like Lee Stafford, VO5 Matte Clay, Fudge and Jonathan Dirt, are used for the peasant look, as well as Vaseline, and dirt powder, which is incidentally a real product.

Talking about dirtying up a garment, Clapton said, 'If it takes three days to make a costume, it then takes another three days to destroy it and break it. After the actors have worn it a few days in the sun it gets even better – nice and ripe!'

Game of Thrones doesn't look like any other fantasy epic, and Clapton puts this down to her refusal to ditch her work ethic. The ageing and breaking-down process of the costumes may be the most time-consuming process at work, but it is what makes the show so different from others that have preceded it.

'When you are shooting in HD, breaking down a costume can't be done too quickly or it will show,' Clapton explained to the *Hollywood Reporter*. 'You spend two weeks breaking down, patching, dying, repatching. Then you trash it, age it, then trash it again and repair. You can't just stick a couple of patches on it and spray it with dirt because that is exactly what it will look like on HD televisions.'

DAVOS SEAWORTH

Liam Cunningham said about the character to *SFX* magazine, 'Davos Seaworth aka – he's probably got the unsexiest title of them all – the Onion Knight. He finds himself in a bizarre position because he was a criminal. Seventeen years before we meet him, there was a battle raging, and Stannis and his associates, family and everybody else, were under siege, starving, literally on death's door, and Davos came in and saved the day with a large boat full of onions and meat. Stannis took him into his employ, made him a knight – hence the Onion Knight – but also he'd broken the law smuggling, so Stannis got out the cleaver and chopped off four of his fingers.'

He continued, 'In a bizarre way, Davos has a certain amount of respect for that. He has a vein running through him of honour and duty and loyalty, and saw the right of that and has become Stannis' right-hand man.'

His heroic gesture happened during Robert's Rebellion. The Storm's End siege took place over a year, and his act allowed Stannis' men to survive until Eddard Stark arrived. Davos agreed to Stannis' punishment as long as Stannis swung the blade himself, and kept the bones in a pouch around his neck as a good-luck gesture, believing it was what had given his family a future.

During Stannis' attempts to overtake King's Landing, Davos becomes part of the Battle of the Blackwater. Stannis' army is destroyed by wildfire, and he is thrown from the boat into the sea, feared dead. However, he is washed up and stranded on the Spears of the Merlin King. When he is rescued, he attempts to kill Melisandre, blaming her for the defeat. Fearing that she would kill another of King Robert's bastards, Edric Storm, as a sacrifice, he smuggled the young one out of Dragonstone.

It was feared that he was captured on the order of Cersei Lannister, with rumours that parts of his body were displayed for all to see. However, a lookalike prisoner was executed in his place.

Fan favourite Davos Seaworth is played by Irish actor Liam Cunningham.

Cunningham is a softly spoken actor but has an authoritative tone and commanding presence. It's no surprise, then, that the *Game of Thrones* bosses were desperate to have him on the show.

'I actually met them the first time around – for various reasons of timing it didn't work out,' he said to *SFX*. 'But they did say, "Look, we've got some really interesting guys coming in next year, please come up and talk to us." Then Davos Seaworth came up and I said, "You bet ya, I'll have some of that." He's not one of the grunts, anything could happen – who knows where this thing is going to go – but at the moment, I spend a lot of time talking and arguing, and trying to be diplomatic. It's slightly more cerebral for the moment.'

Cunningham hinted at what is to come: 'Things do get a little physical towards the end of this season, but I don't want to give too much away,' he said. 'There's an extraordinary climax that comes towards the latter half of the series (two), and the entire front of the series is building up this paranoia. We've got some great stuff coming up, certainly towards the end – Tyrion starts using his noggin that much more, not just to protect himself but to protect the kingdom and protect the throne. As the poster says, war is coming!'

DOTHRAKI LANGUAGE

One of the many tasks that faced Benioff and Weiss was creating a new language for the Dothraki clan – a fearsome group of riders and raiders with their own harsh tongue. They turned to the Language Creation Society to create the sprawling language, asking members to come up with a single proposal – ultimately selecting David J. Peterson's submission.

Drawing on vocabulary from Russia, Turkey, Estonia, Inuktitut and Swahili, he set about the mammoth task.

Peterson said in a statement, released by HBO:

In designing Dothraki, I wanted to remain as faithful as possible to the extant material in George R. R. Martin's series. Though there isn't a lot of data, there is evidence of a dominant word order (subject-verb-object), of adjectives appearing after nouns, and of the lack of a copula (to be). I've remained faithful to these elements, creating a sound aesthetic that will be familiar to readers, while giving the language depth and authenticity. My fondest desire is for fans of the series to look at a word from the Dothraki language and be unable to tell if it came from the books or from me and for viewers not even to realise it's a constructed language.

For his part, Weiss added in the same statement:

> We're tremendously excited to be working with
> David and the LCS. The language he's devised is
> phenomenal. It captures the essence of the Dothraki
> and brings another level of richness to their world.
> We look forward to his first collection of Dothraki
> love sonnets.

Peterson didn't take the task lightly. In Martin's books,
there are some choice words in Dothraki, but Weiss and
Benioff were convinced the series needed an actual
language, and not just some regurgitated mumbo jumbo,
for certain scenes.

He created an extensive database of English to Dothraki
terms, using nearly 2,000 vocabulary words, and recorded
each on to CD so that the cast could hear how each word
should sound. Those actors who would be speaking
Dothraki would learn their language in English at first to
get the pitch and emotion right, before then listening to
the CDs in Dothraki.

Undeterred by learning a whole new language for the
part, Jason Momoa, who plays Drogo, was just desperate to
get started. 'Some of the stuff I say, I've never heard said on
TV or in the movies. So, to top it off with this amazing
language that they've created, it was an honour. I don't

think I'll ever get to play a character like that ever again. It's just fantastic to submerge yourself in this foreign language. I can't speak any other languages, it's English and Dothraki now, but it was a trip.'

Emilia Clarke, who plays Daenerys (Dany), added to *thisisfakediy.com*, 'I remember on the first day filming Dothraki I was beyond petrified. You just have a mind blank when it comes to it. But once you get through that and the words start to become far more familiar you kind of almost just have to turn your brain off and you know it. It just comes out. So yeah, just trying to get some good acting in there as well is the difficult bit!'

A Dothraki day could make for a very long day's filming, she added. 'Basically it is a language that I could be fluent in but I'm not. You get the scripts through and the Dothraki on top of it so you get to kind of map the English onto the Dothraki, find the right intonations and all that kind of stuff, but it's a language and a culture that has come from George's imagination and we're trying to put it on screen, so you kind of have liberty to sort of create it for yourself really as actors. So it was really, really good fun and it was a way of getting into Dany even more, and her world.'

However, creating a new language, unsurprisingly, has its hardships.

On 10 October 2011, Peterson was woken up around

two in the morning. Being woken up wasn't a new thing working on the show, with the production team hastily demanding a translation request despite the time difference, but he believed he had finished with series two.

Recalling the moment on his blog, he said, 'I received an e-mail from Bryan Cogman at 4.03am [his time] entitled "EMERGENCY Dothraki line!!!" He said they needed the Dothraki for "Take all the gold and jewels", and they needed it in a couple hours. Even though it was late, I quickly translated the line and sent it off to Bryan at 1.09pm [their time]. Unfortunately, it did *not*, in fact, make it in time. Bryan wasn't on set that day, but he said he thought they did it in Common language, which is unfortunate (the more Dothraki, the better!), but what could I do? So I chalked that one up to bad luck, and promptly forgot about it.'

However, he was stunned to find months later that Iain Glen had ad-libbed it. Luckily, he was impressed with Glen's attempt and managed to work it in to fit the language that he created.

Glen himself said of the Dothraki language to *westeros.org*, 'They're a nightmare. It's this gobbledygook language that's very, very hard to learn, but it's very much worth the effort because when you try and just make up your own, it always sounds very foolish. This very bright linguist developed this entire language, and so whenever a line is needed he's referred to. He comes up with it, and it's always very consistent. But it's really hard. One line is okay, but if you have a speech, man, it's hard – it's really hard.

'You really just need to learn it by rote. It's this series of nonsense syllables. David says the line for you, so you learn the pattern but he doesn't really do the intonation and he's also American, so it sounds different. But he gives you the right sound. And then you think very clearly about the line in English and how you'd say it as you say the Dothraki line. So if it's a line in Dothraki where you're angry, you'll learn it again and again to get it right.'

A hugely impressed Martin now seeks Peterson's advice while working on the last two books, as he told *Empire*, 'I now consult him when I want to invent a new Dothraki word. He's prepared a dictionary and a lexicon. It's amazing; it added so much to the show to have them speak Dothraki with subtitles rather than just English.

'In 2010, I visited the Jenolan Caves in Australia, and in some of the caves they have self-guided tours where you pick up a headset and get descriptions of what you're looking at. Since this is a big tourist destination they offer these in many languages. One of which is Klingon. I was startled when I saw that. I do wonder how many people choose to take the Klingon tour. But that has now become my ambition, to have the Dothraki language added to that, so we have equality with the damn Klingons.'

DROGO

The Dothraki are a fearsome and incredibly violent nation of raiders. When villagers see their horses coming towards them, they know their end is nigh, with the men killed and women raped. One of them is more feared than most, however.

Drogo is a powerful warlord and a fighter that has never been defeated, which is why Viserys Targaryen conspires for his young sister Daenerys to marry Drogo. The plan is for him to lead his troops against an invasion at the King's Landing, so that eventually Viserys can reclaim the throne he believes belongs to him.

However, despite his mighty façade, Drogo's heart softens towards his new wife and he becomes a kind and compassionate husband. His love for her never burns so brightly than when he learns of a failed assassination attempt on her life. Enraged, he decides to lead the invasion against those who would dare take his pregnant wife away from him.

He ends up killing Viserys because of his lack of respect for his sister, but is later wounded by a fellow Dothraki warrior who challenges his leadership. As a consequence, his wound festers, and, after Daenerys unwisely uses black magic to take the life of her child for that of her fatally wounded husband, she is shocked to discover she was duped – her child is no more and her husband is seemingly brain dead.

Daenerys smothers him out of sympathy and uses his funeral pyre to hatch her dragon eggs, calling her favourite dragon Drogon out of respect for her husband.

For their Drogo, HBO decided on Jason Momoa – a hulking beefcake who had appeared in *Baywatch* and *Stargate: Atlantis*, where he played the role of Ronon Dex for five years. He also starred as the lead in the remake of *Conan the Barbarian*.

Born in Hawaii in 1979, but raised in Iowa, Momoa ended up moving back to the island just before he was 20. It was there that he struck a modelling deal and ended up winning Hawaii's Model of the Year in 1999, leading to his starring in *Baywatch Hawaii* for two years.

He is married to *Cosby Show* star Lisa Bonet, who gave birth to their daughter Lola Iolani Momoa in 2007, with their son Nakoa-Wolf Manakauapo Namakaeha being added to the brood a year later.

In 2008, Momoa's face was slashed with a broken glass at a Hollywood café and he received 140 stitches as a result. A 21-year-old man was arrested and sent to prison for five years. Momoa's scars from the attack are still obvious since the incident.

Landing the part was tough for Momoa, taking seven months between his first and second audition. However, when he came back to read for the character, he knew exactly how to channel the ferocious power of Drogo. When he performed the intimidating Haka war dance, a routine that New Zealand's All Blacks do before a game, it frightened the life out of the casting agent.

'It's a war chant,' he said to *Den of Geek*, 'I just thought, in the scenes I was doing, you don't get a sense of what this warrior's like. What it would be like if he was commanding his officers, or what he'd be like in battle. I wanted to represent that and channel a little bit of my ancestry and heritage. I'm half Hawaiian.'

Momoa explained what awaited the agents: 'I went into HBO and I said, "Don't be scared or anything, but when you're in front of a large man doing the Haka, you're going to feel it. You're going to feel some energy coming at you."

'These two little white women were like, "Holy shit." People were coming out of their doors and wondering what was going on. It really sealed the deal. And it got me Conan. It's a great way to start an audition. My heart was racing, and I'm sure theirs were, too.'

He was clearly excited about the part, adding, 'I read the book. I had two days and I was hooked. Right after the audition, I read the whole thing, and it's so great, the way you invest in these characters. You think, in the first few episodes, my character's just this intimidating badass, but you slowly watch him fall in love and see how frail he is compared to this stoic; you compare him to the other characters, who are meant to be the good guys, and you think they're totally the opposite. There's such richness to these characters.'

When he attended a screening of the first episode with his wife, he warned her that she wouldn't like what she saw. The whole episode paints Drogo as a grunting man beast and a warrior who watches with glee other people suffering, and he barely carries a thought as he roughly beds his new wife on their wedding day.

'I didn't want my wife to see *Game of Thrones* and she ended up becoming obsessed,' he told *Starpulse*. 'She was dreaming about it, she was so obsessed. We didn't go to the premiere. I was like, "I don't do anything but do [have sex with] Emilia Clarke for the first two episodes. I don't even speak. We don't need to go."'

It shouldn't have just been his wife that he was concerned about – audiences were turned off by his performance in the debut episode. He was too rough and ready, they said, with many mocking his 'guy-liner' look.

However, as the series went on, more and more became enraptured by Momoa, as Drogo evolved from the one-note warrior to a man in love. His passing became one of the moving deaths in the series, and fans took to Twitter to mourn his death. Luckily for them, he came back for the end of series two in a cameo appearance, and no one was more pleased than his screen wife, Emilia Clarke, who dubs him her 'big brother'.

EMILIA CLARKE

Born in 1987, Emilia Clarke is a young actress best known for her career-making role as Daenerys Targaryen. Alongside Tyrion Lannister, Daenerys is George R. R. Martin's favourite creation from the books, and it's not hard to see why.

Her character's transformation as the series develops is a startling one, and it required an actress capable of excelling as both a shy girl and later a fierce and loyal leader.

When she is first introduced in the series, Daenerys is meek and completely dependent on her brother, Viserys. He treats his sister as a toy, something malleable for him to manipulate at will and which he can subject to his mood swings, and his cruel and violent streak. And while Daenerys would burn with the same obsession as her brother – the belief that the Iron Throne was their denied birthright – it was Viserys who held this belief from the start.

Daenerys is the only daughter of King Aerys II – the Mad King – and was conceived shortly before Robert's Rebellion that ended her father's reign on the Iron Throne. Her father died before her birth, with her mother dying just after labour, and she was born at her family's ancestral seat, Dragonstone. She and her brother were smuggled from Dragonstone garrison before they could be turned over to Robert's soldiers, and were instead taken to the Free City of Braavos. They were eventually forced out of their home, and took to wandering the nine Free Cities in a bid to find support for Viserys' attempt to wrestle back the throne.

However, Viserys' desperation amuses many, and he is dubbed The Beggar King. That is, until they find what they want in Pentos, with a powerful Magister named Illyrio Mopatis helping them to reclaim their royal honour. Viserys hatches a plan with Illyrio to marry Daenerys to Khal Drogo, the brutal leader of the Dothraki clan, in the hope that he will lead his army against the King.

In the books, the character is far younger than the one

portrayed in the series – something that shocked Clarke. 'Whilst it's not set in a specific time period because it's fantastical, it's kind of loosely based around what you may believe to be social situations in medieval times,' she said to *heyyouguys.co.uk*. 'In that sense, everything was younger, people died younger, so it's less shocking in terms of that. But at the same time, it just proves that she's more of a complex, incredible character that she came to those realisations so young.'

During the wedding, she receives three dragon eggs from Illyrio – merely decorative symbolic stones, as dragons were believed to be extinct. Westeros knight Jorah Mormont offers both books and his service.

Because Daenerys is something of a nomad herself, she feels beholden to her new family – and stands up to her bullying brother, before eventually watching him die at the hands of her husband, Drogo.

After the death of her beloved Drogo, she constructs a funeral pyre for his body, placing her dragon eggs near his body and stepping on to the blazing fire. Jorah is convinced it's suicide, but she knows differently, strongly believing she has a connection with the dragons. And her instincts are right – the following morning she is alive with three hatched dragons clinging to her charred body.

As her dragons grow, so do the tales around the Seven Kingdoms, leading to a whole host of danger that comes with owning such prized creatures. After seeking shelter and barely escaping with their lives in the Qarth, she looks to find more support for her attempt to win back her believed birthright.

'I just think of her getting stronger and stronger,' said Clarke. 'She gets her trust boundaries tested to the max in season two, so in that sense it's intriguing. She's coming up with having to deal with [being] not only a woman, but a young girl in a man's world, in a male-orientated society that she has to come up against, and even having dragons doesn't seem to make a huge amount of difference.'

SPOILER

Without Drogo, and with only Jorah's words to comfort her, Daenerys begins to grow tired of Jorah's advances and of him thinking of her as only a child, so she sets out her claim as a kind but strong leader – using her dragons against those cities who use slaves, and asserting her leadership over Jorah.

Unsurprisingly, there are people that would like her killed, and she is only saved from an assassination attempt by a man named Arstan Whitebeard – who ends up being famed knight Barristan Selmy. Exiled from his Kingsguard duties by Cersei Lannister, he seeks Daenerys out as the true queen of the Seven

---

Kingdoms. He also tells her that Jorah was once a spy for Varys at the Red Keep, keeping him informed of Daenerys' movements.

She sends them both on an apparent suicide mission during the Siege of Meeren, and when they both survive Selmy apologises for his duplicity. Jorah is less pleading, however, and, while she wants to pardon him, she has no choice but to banish her former right-hand man.

Word quickly starts to spread around Westeros of a young queen with dragons. However, after a six-year-old girl is believed to have been killed by one of her dragons, she orders them to be locked below ground to prevent any more similar deaths. But one of them, Drogon, named after her beloved husband, escapes.

She marries again in a bid to quell the wars that rage around her as she attempts to get the boats to lead her army to King's Landing. Ending the slave trade has destroyed the economies of several Free Cities, and as such there is much diplomacy needed for her to survive. When Drogon appears in a gladiatorial pit marked for her honour, he is wounded by an animal handler. However, she rushes to his defence, mounting him and then flying away.

For Clarke, it wasn't a part that came easily – the role was originally played by another actress in the un-aired pilot before she was eventually cast as Daenerys.

'I was only aware of it when we got down to the final stages really, that they had already cast someone who was in a pilot that was only seen internally,' Clarke said to *heyyouguys.co.uk.*

'Once they decided to give the whole show the go-ahead, they decided to do a number of recasts, including Dany [Daenerys] as a character.'

Clarke was born in London, and quickly showed an interest in acting after seeing the musical *Show Boat* on stage, where her father worked as a theatre sound engineer. She studied at the Drama Centre London, and eventually landed a small-screen role in an episode of the soap *Doctors* in 2009, and then in 2010's Syfy movie *Triassic Attack*.

Clarke remarked, 'I told my parents I wanted to be an actor and they were getting ready for a life of unemployment so they're just happy I'm in work!'

She then landed the role in *Game of Thrones*. 'My life is pretty much unrecognisable to what it was before. It's incredible!' she said to *heyyouguys.co.uk.* 'Never in a million years did I think I'd be doing something like this now, this early on so fresh out of drama school. Even having *Game of Thrones*, I never knew that it would be the success that it was, and hopefully will continue to be.

'They took a massive risk with me. I had a couple of auditions then a screen-test in LA and then they gave me the part. It was as simple as that, there's no huge story to tell.'

She says about her character, 'I think first and foremost she's a survivalist, and she knows what she needs to do to survive. Unlike many other characters in the show, she doesn't have an egotistical need or desire or want for the Iron Throne; it's something that is her destiny, that she genuinely doesn't have any control over. "Heavy is the head that wears the crown" – if she didn't have to do it then she probably wouldn't. In terms of that, she just realises what her options are and has to make an incredibly difficult choice. I have a problem with her using her sexuality. It's more she knows what she has to do and, as a result of that, finds the love that she finds with Khal [Drogo] and grows in confidence.'

FANTASY

For a long time, fantasy has been seen either as silly stories about monsters or a genre packed with stories so mammoth and dense that viewers or readers needed an encyclopaedia of that world to understand what is going on.

These fantastical worlds often featured even more fantastical characters and genre stereotypes. But Peter Jackson's *Lord of the Rings* changed that. Based on J. R. R. Tolkien's epic trilogy, Jackson's films were triumphs in every sense. A triumph in getting made in the first place (not many studios will agree to filming three fantasy films back to back with a director pretty new to the Hollywood blockbuster lark), a box-office triumph and an Oscar triumph. It changed fantasy overnight.

Ian Bogost, Professor of Digital Media at Georgia Institute of Technology, told CNN that *The Lord of the Rings* was the start of making fantasy mainstream. 'Probably Peter Jackson is to blame,' he said. 'This is all really about Peter Jackson. The hugely successful *Lord of the Rings* movies not only taught untrained viewers how to watch epic fantasy on the big screen, it also proved to Hollywood that fantasy could be a viable mass-market genre. The *Lord of the Rings* films are 10 years old at this point, and they were incredibly lucrative. That's what it takes – an investment that shows that the private sector will go and watch these.'

But, until the success of *Game of Thrones* and *The Lord of the Rings*, fantasy was something in the shadows. As Jackson said himself during a commentary of the film, he doesn't like magic. Instead, characters take precedence.

Author Martin agreed, saying, 'If you look at *The Lord of the Rings*, although Middle Earth is suffused with a great feel of magic, there is very little onstage. Gandalf doesn't shoot lightning bolts from his fingers. If it's on every page, then magic loses its magic.'

Another huge fantasy influence was *The Wheel of Time* – an epic book series that gave the fantasy literary genre a bolt of energy. It was planned to be only six novels but, as Martin knows only so well, it had to be extended. There will be 14 books in the series, excluding companion and prequel novels. Robert Jordan, real name Jim Rigney, began writing the first instalment in 1984, and it was published six years later.

The reason fans are so obsessed with Martin's mortality is that Jordan died in 2007 as he was working on the final book. Luckily, he had planned in advance for such a morbid scenario, and had provided extensive notes for another author to finish his work. To read more about fans' obsession with Martin's mortality, read the section 'A Song of Ice and Fire'.

Fantasy author Brandon Sanderson was assigned the task, and the final book would eventually be made into a trilogy. Selling nearly 50 million copies worldwide, the mammoth book series focuses on the Dark One, the embodiment of pure evil, as he escapes from his prison. One man learns that he is the Messiah, and must do everything he can, no matter the price, to destroy the Dark One.

Robert Jordan was someone that Martin not only admired but also counted as a friend, saying, 'He gave me a blurb when my series was starting out, an endorsement for the cover that got me a lot of readers. And his own work really made my series possible. Jordan essentially broke the trilogy template that Tolkien helped set up. He showed us how to do a book that's bigger than a trilogy. I don't think my series would've been possible without *The Wheel of Time* being as successful as it was. I've always wanted to sprawl, and Jordan, to a great extent, made that possible with his series.'

When Jordan died, Martin wrote the following words on his blog:

The world of high fantasy is poorer today. James Rigney, better known to fantasy readers as Robert Jordan, has passed away. Although he had been fighting amyloidosis for several years, the news of his death still came as a shock to many, including me. He was so optimistic and determined that you had to think that if anyone could beat the disease, it would be him. Jim was a good and gracious man, a pleasure to share a platform or a pint with, and his contributions to modern fantasy were many. His huge, ambitious *Wheel of Time* series helped to redefine the genre, and opened many doors for the writers who followed.

He was also unfailingly generous towards other fantasists, always ready to offer them support and encouragement. My own *Ice & Fire* series might never have found its audience without the cover quote that

Jim was so kind as to provide, back when *A Game of Thrones* was first published. I will always be grateful to him for that.

G

GARY LIGHTBODY

Gary Lightbody is the lead singer of the British alternative rock band Snow Patrol and is a huge fan of the series. So the singer was delighted when he filmed a small cameo for season three.

Dressed in medieval gear, he took to the band's Facebook page to share a photo of himself on set. He wrote, 'So I did my scene this morning for *Game of Thrones*. I looked like this. Can't say much, just it's no pivotal role. Fun!'

The Irish singer regularly hangs out with some of the cast when they film in Belfast and even has Twitter conversations with fans of the show.

Gary has been a member of Snow Patrol since 1994, and they have had two massive hit songs: 'Run', which was covered by Leona Lewis, whose version reached number one in the UK charts, and 'Chasing Cars'.

GEORGE R. R. MARTIN

Ironically, George Raymond Richard Martin turned to writing fantasy epics because his imagination was hampered by TV. The television veteran grew frustrated by the constraints, complaining, 'My scripts were always too long, they were always too expensive. I was always having to cut them. There were too many characters, too many matte paintings. We can't have all these matte paintings; we can't have this giant battle scene that you've written because we can only afford 12 extras.

'So when I went back to books, I said, "I don't care about any of that any more. I'm going to write a story that's going to be as gigantic a story as I want. I'm going to have hundreds of characters, gigantic battles, magnificent castles and vistas; all the things I couldn't do in television, I'm going to do in these books, and I hope people like it." So now here we are doing it for television. But fortunately it's David and Dan [Benioff and Weiss] who have to figure out all the problems, not me.'

Martin was born in New Jersey on 20 September 1948

in a federal housing project near to the Bayonne docks. It was clear from a young age that he possessed a wild imagination, selling monster stories to neighbourhood children to earn pennies. After some of his pet turtles died, he penned a tale of a mythical kingdom, where his turtles killed each other to rise to power.

I had a world that was five blocks long,' he told *Rolling Stone* magazine. 'My house was on First Street and my school was on Fifth Street. But my imagination wanted a world that was much bigger than that. So I would read about distant planets and ancient Rome and Shanghai and Gotham City.'

He devoured superhero comics, particularly the Silver Age Marvel ones, which are credited with adding a sense of realism and a more human perspective than the invulnerable and slightly dull ones that preceded them. The avid collector has a huge comic-book collection, including the first issues of *Spider-Man* and *Fantastic Four*.

After obtaining conscientious objector status to avoid the Vietnam War, he studied journalism, while also continuing to write – eventually carving out a successful career. He was nominated for two prestigious Hugo Awards, although he did not go on to win them. In 1976, he helped organise the first annual Hugo Losers Party.

The surprise failure of 1983's *The Armageddon Rag* 'essentially destroyed my career as a novelist at the time',

Martin admitted. 'Growing up poor as I did, a kid from the projects of Bayonne, New Jersey, I'm always conscious of the way money can go away. Back when I sold *The Armageddon Rag*, it took me about a year to write and I got $100,000 for it. And when that happened, I said to myself, "I now make $100,000 a year." And that was a huge mistake. I bought a house and a new car, and then the book failed to sell at all. We had to get a second mortgage, and I thought, "How am I going to make my payments?"'

He turned to TV, which saw him hired to revive *The Twilight Zone* and for a new working of classic story *Beauty and the Beast*, which starred *Terminator* actress Linda Hamilton. In 1987, his novella *Nightflyers* was adapted into a feature film with the same name.

Talking about his time in Hollywood to the *Chicago Tribune*, he said, 'There were things about it I loved, and there were things about it I hated. But what was very good about those five years was that I was part of a writing staff, the writing and producing staff on shows that were actually on the air. I would write a script and we would rewrite it and sometimes there would be fights with the network or the studio or the censors. But in the end, the fight would be resolved and then the show would go before the camera and then a couple of weeks later it would be on the air and millions of people would see it.'

However, it was when he started developing his own

series that he began to grow frustrated by the process, adding, 'And that was the process that I sort of got used to. But the second five years that I was out there, I had reached the point where I was doing pilots. I was doing feature films. I was doing development. I had an overall deal at Columbia, and you know they call it development hell for a reason. I found myself writing scripts and sometimes working on something for a year or maybe two years and pouring my heart and soul into it, creating good things and then, "No, we're not going to do that one. No, the other network is doing something similar. Oh, we have another show we like better." So you're paid a great deal of money, but four guys in the room are the only people who ever saw it.

'I decided I just couldn't do that anymore. It was just too psychologically frustrating. It certainly drove me crazy. And probably the most frustrating was the pilot that got the closest to being done.'

He went on to explain, 'I did a show called *Doorways* that was the only one of my pilots that was actually filmed, and everybody loved it. It was for ABC, and it was going to go on the air; they ordered six backup scripts, which was a huge order for backup scripts then. Then there were personnel changes and some executives left and other executives were promoted, and suddenly we weren't on the air. And suddenly I was back to square one. And I did a few more pilots and all that, but the failure of *Doorways* to get on the air kind of took the heart out of me.'

Martin then explained how this disappointment turned him back to writing books, saying, 'Books had always been my first love anyway. So at that point I started writing what would eventually be *A Game of Thrones*.'

GREYJOY REBELLION

Nine years before the beginning of events in *Game of Thrones*, and six years after the victory of Robert's Rebellion, a rising led by Balon Greyjoy attempted to break away from the Seven Kingdoms for independence for the Iron Islands.

Greyjoy was unsure about King Robert; he believed he lacked support, and prepared himself for war against the Iron Throne – starting with a surprise attack at Lannisport, burning the Lannister fleet at anchor, and embarking on several smaller raids around the surrounding coastlines.

The counter-attack by Robert was swift and strong. Supervised by his brother Stannis, his army and resources outnumbered Greyjoy's – and they significantly hindered the rebellion – destroying the Iron Fleet near Fair Isle.

Robert and Lord Eddard Stark were reunited in battle at Pyke, the main battle of the Greyjoy rebellion. Jorah Mormont was also there that day, and was rewarded with a knighthood for his bravery. Jaime Lannister was there, too, and the battle also featured the iconic image of Thoros of Myr leading the attack with a sword covered in wildfire.

The battle was fierce and long, with the castle eventually being taken by the King and Balon Greyjoy eventually forced to swear loyalty to the Iron Throne. His only surviving son, Theon, was taken into the care of Ned Stark to ensure a rebellion didn't happen again.

Theon Greyjoy – played by Alfie Allen – is a complicated character. Despite being raised with honour and kindness by Ned, he is still in effect a hostage, and is torn between his new family and the old one that left him behind.

Allen said about the character to GQ magazine, 'I don't think people are going to like him as much as other characters in the show. But that doesn't matter because as long as you feel sympathy for him, and why he does all these horrible things, then I feel like I've achieved what I set out to do.

'I always set out to do that, really, to make people feel sorry for him and understand why he did what he does.'

He went on to explain the differences between the character in the book and the TV series: 'In the book it starts out and it seems like he's almost set out to betray Robb from the start, which doesn't paint him in a nice light. In the series, we approached it differently, showing all the decisions that lead him down that way and that they're due to the humiliation and rejection he receives from his family. He's absolutely desperate for the approval of his father. And I think once he realises that that's a lost cause, he tries to prove it to himself that he can hold Winterfell, can hold that power and authority, but what he's really doing is ruling through fear. It's not the first time that someone's gone about it that way before. It's a strong character trait of his that, to be respected, he has to disrespect other people.'

He added, 'He has love, he has it in his heart, but that means he wants to be loved and he's never really gotten it. Ned Stark's probably put his arm around his shoulder at some point, but he's never really taught him the right and wrong way of life, and apart from Ned he never really had a role model. That's where the conflict comes in his mind; this mental torture happens because no one is telling him right from wrong. He's crying out for someone to tell him what to do, and he never really gets it and that's why he makes so many brash decisions. If you're going to tell a lie, tell a big one – you know what I mean?'

H

HAND OF THE KING

By the end of season one, we see two Hands of the King take up the position separately, and both are dead before the final season. It may be a prestigious position, one where you are the chief adviser to the King of the realm, but it is also one that carries the threat of danger.

The official duties are drafting laws and commanding the King's armies but also maintaining the day-to-day work of the kingdom. But, in reality, it's about playing games, massaging egos and undertaking constant damage control with the Small Council. As such, the rewards are small but the punishments severe. No wonder one of the sayings that describes the position is: 'The King eats, and the Hand takes the shit.'

When Robert Baratheon is King, he had two Hands, but obviously not at the same time – Jon Arryn and Lord Eddard Stark.

Arryn is only seen for a few seconds briefly in episode one, but he is one of the most important characters – as it is his death that sets off the events of the entire series. He was like a father to Eddard and Robert as Warden of the East, and, when the Mad King wanted them to be turned over, he refused, fighting several Lords over the decision. He fought on Robert's side during his attempt to take over the throne, and married Lysa Tully in a bid to gain her father's powerful support.

After Robert took the crown, he made his 'second' father the Hand. Arryn advised Robert to marry Cersei Lannister, believing that a cemented alliance with Tywin Lannister would ensure that finance would never be an issue. However, Robert would still spend an extravagant amount of money on tournaments.

Arryn and Stannis Baratheon later figure out that Robert was not the father to Cersei's children; it was, in fact, Jaime Lannister, her brother. Arryn was killed before he could tell anyone else the news. The second Hand, Ned Stark, is beheaded near the end of series one.

In series two, Tywin Lannister is King Joffrey's Hand,

with Tyrion acting Hand. Tyrion plays an integral part in the Battle of Blackwater but is not really credited for the victory and is soon replaced by his father.

SPOILER

When Tommen Baratheon becomes King, Tywin Lannister, Harys Swyft, Orton Merryweather and Mace Tyrell have all been his Hand.

HBO

The year 2010 saw, as *Entertainment Weekly* described it, a miraculous recovery for HBO – aka Home Box Office. The company had been hit by accusations that the trailblazing network credited for injecting new life into tired US dramas and sitcoms had lost its mojo.

But that year showed impressive signs that it was back. *True Blood* was hugely popular for it, as was comedy *Eastbound & Down*. It also had *Treme*, from the writers of *The Wire*, and *Boardwalk Empire* – the searing prohibition drama that was produced by Hollywood legend Martin Scorsese.

It also had *Game of Thrones*, albeit only as a pilot, but already heat was building up about the project.

HBO's programming president, Michael Lombardo, found the storytelling more appealing than the low-key magic or the exotic milieu, despite the network's new developmental policy to 'take shots at shows that we wouldn't have taken a shot at five years ago'. In August 2010, Lombardo made an unusual confession – he didn't particularly care for fantasy stories: 'It wasn't the genre we responded to, it was the storytelling,' he said. 'There's enormous pressure on the *Game of Thrones* people. It's a very sophisticated audience; you have to get it right.'

There were comparisons with *True Blood*, with HBO executive Richard Plepler admitting, 'Alan [Ball, creator of *True Blood*,] has created this extremely compelling and addictive world. When you get passionate fan bases, they talk with each other and that's catalytic.'

HBO has nearly 30 million subscribers, and broadcasts to over 150 countries. The network's origins go back to 1965, when Charles Dolan won a franchise to build a cable system in New York, which became the first urban underground cable system in the US. Calling it the Sterling Manhattan Cable, he laid the cable underneath the streets because the large buildings blocked TV signals. Time-Life, a production company, bought a 20 per cent stake in the company, agreeing to back Dolan's idea of the Green Channel – which would become HBO in November 1972.

The pay-for channel showed films and sporting events, but it would constantly lose customers, who grew weary of watching the same films and subsequently cancelled their subscription. However, the channel would continue to innovate with satellite technology and original programming, including HBO's first made-for-pay-TV movie aired in 1983. Time Inc merged with Warner Communications in 1989, and HBO is now a part of Time Warner.

The turnaround in fortune, and a sign of things to come, came with *The Larry Sanders Show* in 1992. Starring Gary Shandling, the fly-on-the-wall comedy/drama of a late-night television show was a major success, winning awards, and it clearly influenced other HBO comedy shows like *Curb Your Enthusiasm*. Because it's a subscription-only service, there is more freedom to use explicit content such as profanity and nudity.

HBO's first one-hour drama series was prison drama *Oz*, and they followed that up with *The Sopranos*. The mafia drama would run to six seasons and become part of pop culture. Scoring an astonishing 111 Emmy nominations, the show has been praised for its dark content and well-drawn characters. There is no right or wrong, and the narrative structure, normally so tight and rigid when it comes to episode TV, is fluid and loose. There wasn't always an explosive third act and a reveal could happen any time, not just as the end credits rolled – a formula that had served TV for decades. People died when you least expected it and the main characters didn't learn moral lessons at the end.

More impressive shows followed, but they broke new grounds once again in 2002 with *The Wire*. A slow burner in every sense, the show, about Baltimore cops tackling, in vain, the drug culture that permeates the city from the very top to the very bottom, took a while to get going, and even longer to get an audience.

But there comes a point when the show clicks: it could be the simple shot of D'Angelo playing chess in the middle of a council estate or Jimmy McNulty encouraging his children to spy on a prominent drug dealer in an outdoor market. But, when it does, *The Wire* is pure TV addiction – each episode layered with so much love and detail in the characters that frequent this realistic world. The show would eventually find an audience, and they would become ardent supporters, spreading the word to anyone who listened.

HBO continues to roll out programmes of the highest order – most recently *Boardwalk Empire* and *True Blood*. And, of course, *Game of Thrones*.

One of the criticisms levelled at HBO is that it doesn't do enough to tackle piracy. *Game of Thrones* is one of the most pirated shows in the US. According to Forbes' Andy Greenberg, 'The second season of the show has been downloaded more than 25 million times from public torrent trackers since it began in early April, and its piracy hit a new peak following 30 April's episode, with more than 2.5 million downloads in a day.'

Season one was the most pirated show of all time, behind season six of *Dexter*.

'HBO hasn't helped the problem by making the show tough to watch online for the young and cable-less,' notes Greenberg. 'The show isn't available through Hulu or Netflix, iTunes offers only season one, and using HBO's own streaming site HBO Go requires a cable subscription.'

I

ILLYRIO MOPATIS

Illyrio Mopatis resides in the Free City of Pentos. He is a rich man thanks to his dealings in a range of spices and dragon bones. He and Varys concocted a scheme whereby Varys would steal precious objects from thieves, and Illyrio would retrieve them for their previous owners for a small fee. It would make them very rich, and their wealth would continue to grow through his very first spy network.

Mopatis' main aim is to find a way for the exiled Targaryens to reclaim their place on the Iron Throne and is using Varys' influence as the Kingdom's master whisperer to achieve that.

Obese, with a yellow stained beard, Mopatis used to be an exceptionally handsome Sellsword. He has a daily reminder of that time, with a marble statue of him as a naked boy, lithe and handsome, adorning his marble pool. He is close to crying when he sees the difference between the way he looked as a young boy compared to how he is now.

It was at his home that he watched over Viserys and Daenerys Targaryen, after agreeing to take them in, but it is revealed that he once thought of killing Viserys so that he could marry his young sister, Daenerys. But he soon realised her timid nature would not be a suitable match for him.

His protection over them seems to stem from a monetary interest rather than true love, as Viserys is said to have promised him the Master of Coin title when he became King. In return, Mopatis massages Viserys' ego by telling him that Westeros are desperate for him to return and toasts his victory. He is also the person that brokered the arranged marriage between Daenerys and Khal Drogo.

IRON THRONE

It may not look the most comfy of chairs, with its jagged edges, twisted metal, spikes and hard surface, but the Iron

Throne is the greatest seat in Westeros. It's the seat of the Kings, and the whole saga of *A Song of Ice and Fire* series is about who will finally sit upon it.

The throne is made from a thousand swords surrendered by Aegon the Conqueror's enemies. Aegon Targaryen was the first King of the Seven Kingdoms, and Balerion the Dragon heated and melted down the blades. He made it as uncomfortable as possible, ruling that a king should never sit easy. The Mad King (Aerys II Targaryen) is said to have cut himself several times.

Mark Addy, who plays King Robert, said, 'I didn't actually shoot any scenes in what is the Throne Room where the Iron Throne is, but we did a poster shoot and that was the only time I actually sat on the Iron Throne. It was interesting because you sat on it and went, "Oh this is not very comfy," and the designers went, "Ha ha! Exactly!" because of course it's not the place that you want to be. Whoever's on the Iron Throne, you are right in the firing line there.'

The Throne Room was decorated with skulls of dragons, but Robert got rid of them in favour of hunting tapestries. The Throne is said to have killed several people, with the Throne Room the setting for the death of Richard and Brandon Stark, and Joffrey during his wedding feast.

SPOILER

The current King to sit on the Iron Throne is Tommen Baratheon following the death of his older brother, Joffrey.

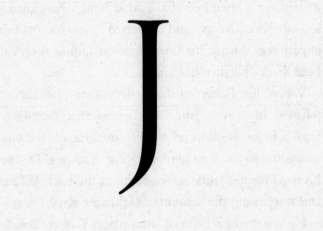

JAIME LANNISTER

The bad boy of Westeros, Jaime Lannister is a handsome, long-haired blond, with a swaggering machismo and a quick tongue. He is capable of doing the most dastardly of things to get his way. So the fact that he garners, if not sympathy, a sense of empathy is a great credit to Martin's writing and Danish actor Nikolaj Coster-Waldau's performance.

Jaime Lannister, more commonly known as the Kingslayer, is the first-born son of Tywin Lannister, arriving shortly after his twin sister Cersei. As Hand to the King, at 15 years old Jaime became the youngest person in history to become a member of the Mad King's Kingsguard. He served King Aerys, and watched a series of horrific encounters during his time there including the death of Ned Stark's brother and father.

When his father stormed the castle and raped and pillaged the town, Jaime discovered that the King had buried huge amounts of wildfire underneath the city and was going to use it to blow up King's Landing. Disobeying his royal pledge, Jaime stabbed him in the back, killing him and warranting the unwanted nickname Kingslayer.

He watched his beloved sister marry Robert Baratheon, and she would have three children during their marriage. However, the children, Joffrey, Myrcella and Tommen, are not, in fact, Robert's but Jaime's. The twins had been inseparable growing up, and had begun to sexually experiment together when they were younger.

During one such incident, they are discovered by a servant who quickly tells their mother. As a result, she moves them to separate sides of the castles and forbids them from ever doing it again – something that obviously didn't work.

Jaime leaves home at 11 to be a squire, but at 15 he visits his sister. While visiting her, he is told by Cersei that their father wants him to marry Lysa Tully, so she comes up with a plan that will see Jaime become a member of the Kingsguard, believing that this will keep them closer together and avoid Jaime being married off to another woman. They end up having sex and Cersei makes sure that he becomes a member of the royal order.

Jaime soon realises that the Mad King has only chosen him for the honour to get back at his father, of whom Aerys was jealous – robbing him of the chance to make his favourite son heir to Casterly Rock.

Their mother wasn't the only person to discover Jaime and Cersei's incest – Bran Stark discovers the pair having sex, while he is climbing an outbuilding. The consequence for Bran is life changing: Jaime throws him out of the window and, although he survives the massive fall, he is left a cripple. This incident triggers the divide between the Lannisters and the Starks, eventually leading to Jaime's capture by Robb Stark's army. On top of this, while remaining under Robb's watch, unbeknown to Jaime, his beloved sister has begun a sexual relationship with their cousin, Lancel.

After being held prisoner by the Starks for some time, Jaime is eventually released by Catelyn Stark, an unlikely hero. Acting on her own behalf for the love of her family, and against Robb's command, she wants to make an exchange for her two daughters. Catelyn doesn't act in haste, though, and entrusts a fearsome female warrior named Brienne to take him back to King's Landing with her terms. During their journey home, Jaime eventually warms to Brienne, even though he finds her one of the ugliest maids he has ever set his eyes upon.

SPOILER

The journey back to King's Landing is long, and on their way back they are captured. Their captors recognise Jaime straight away and taunt him for being the Kingslayer. As a punishment, they cut off his sword hand, leaving him with a rotting stump, and take him to Harrenhal as a captor. After he sinks into a deep depression on realising that the only thing that made him the fearsome man he was was his sword hand, it is Brienne who helps him recover. Eventually, Jaime is freed, but Brienne remains imprisoned. However, while making his way home, Jaime has a moving dream about her and heads back to Harrenhal to rescue his companion.

After returning to King's Landing, and following the death of Joffrey, Jaime meets up again with Cersei and they have sex right in front of their son's corpse. However, Jaime has returned a changed man, and his relationship with Cersei falls apart soon after.

When Tyrion is wrongly accused of murdering Joffrey – and sentenced to death – Jaime rescues him.

He also learns that Cersei has been having affairs

behind his back, and when, after leaving King's Landing, he receives a letter from Cersei pleading with him to be her champion in a potential trial-by-combat ruling after she is imprisoned, he orders the letter to be burned.

JON SNOW

While season one is played like an old-fashioned murder mystery, with Ned Stark desperately seeking answers as to who killed his mentor Jon Arryn, there is a far deeper mystery at hand that is still to be resolved – who is Jon Snow's mother?

The bastard son of Eddard Stark is a tag that Snow has been branded with, and one that makes him bristle from the many remarks that come his way. He wears the insults like a wounded soldier; they keep him in check and make sure he never feels too important.

Raised by his father, he forms a likeable bond with his brother and sisters but meets resistance from their mother, Catelyn Stark. To her, his presence is a daily reminder of her beloved husband's infidelity. She treats him coldly, and his warm relationship with her children upsets her.

Kit Harington, who plays Jon, said about their relationship to *westeros.org*, 'I think he's given up on it. It's not a question that goes away, obviously he wants to know, and we want to know who his mother is, but that's the hard thing about his father's death.'

Not only has Jon lost his father; he's also lost his mother, because the day that Ned died so did his mother's identity. 'So unless Catelyn knows – and she's never going to tell him, and is he never going to see her again – so the question of his mother's identity is forsaken; he can't learn any more,' Harington explained.

'It's never going to happen, that they'll reconcile. I think, from the word go, it was hatred. Well, he didn't hate her, but she hated him.'

Believing his calling to be that of the Night's Watch, Snow had heard tales of a noble breed of warriors who help protect the North from wildings and other creatures. He longed to serve there, seeing it as a chance to carve out his own identity for himself, find a new family and not be tarred with the same brush as his namesake.

He joins the Watch but takes time to settle in, realising that the notion of noble soldiers was a lie. Delinquents are rounded up and are given the choice of maiming, death or a place at Castle Black to serve as part of the Night's Watch. Nevertheless, he quickly realises that this is the family he was searching for.

Snow is assigned to a scouting party in the mountains with a task to kill former Night's Watch member Mance Rayder – the King-Beyond-the-Wall. While out Beyond the Wall, one of his tasks is to take out a group of wilding sentries, one being a woman. His reluctance to kill her sees her managing to escape. He eventually captures her again, but he has lost the other members of the scouting party.

However, when the wildings capture him and one of the other scouting party members, Jon is told by the Night's Watch man to kill him and go undercover to discover the wilding's plans.

SPOILER

Separated from his Night's Watch, Snow meets up with Mance Rayder, and over time he learns of the King-Beyond-the-Wall's plans to invade the Seven Kingdoms. He also becomes the lover of Ygritte, the woman he was supposed to kill, breaking the Night's Watch vows of chastity.

After spending a lot of time with Mance Rayder and the wildings, Snow manages to escape and heads to Castle Black; he sees off the wilding raiders – including Ygritte, who dies in his arms.

They hold the wall for several days, but, when Alliser Thorne and Janos Slynt arrive at Castle Black, he is arrested for his defection. Snow is eventually released from prison and ends up growing into his position as a leader. However, he is stabbed seemingly to death by his fellow commanders because of his

---

insubordination and willingness to team up the Watch with wildings.

We still don't know who his mother is – with possible suspects including Ashara Dayne and a wet nurse called Wylla – but one popular theory is that Ned Stark isn't his father after all. He was, in fact, protecting Jon under the pretence that he is his dad. If that's the case, it limits who his dad could be – with Rhaegar Targaryen often mooted. Rhaegar was the son of the Mad King, and is alleged to have kidnapped Lyanna Stark – Ned's sister, who Robert Baratheon was betrothed to. This would kick-start the events leading to Robert's Rebellion, but there are some who believe that Rhaegar hadn't kidnapped her but, in fact, loved her.

Robert's loathing of all things Targaryen was never better seen when he was presented with the bodies of Rhaegar's dead children after he won his battle against the Mad King. With Ned disgusted at the thought that these kids were slain, Robert was almost happy.

If his beloved Lyanna did fall pregnant with Rhaegar, who knows what Robert would do. And so it would stand to reason that Ned would pretend the child was his, despite having his wife believe he had an affair, if he knew the baby of his sister would come to harm.

Jon Snow is played by Kit Harington.

Kit Harington's life changed when he starred in the original London stage production of *War Horse*, which would eventually become a motion picture by Steven Spielberg.

He said about his character to *westeros.org*, 'When I first got the part, I devoured the books and ended up far, far ahead of myself. They're page-turners. But I had to reel it back in because I was just too far ahead. I really like having the source material there – some actors don't, some actors just want to know it's in the script, but if I have the character there on paper and it has more than what's in the TV script, I want to know.'

Harington continued, 'He did want to know who his mother is, but it isn't what makes him tick; it's that he wants to prove that he's more than a bastard. He's a good man, like his father, and he wants to prove it. He knows he may see his brothers and sisters again, he may see the South again, he may avenge his father's death, but right now he's with the Night's Watch and there he can rise and be the best.

'He's always making mistakes, Jon, because he's trying too hard to impress. He's very good at what he does and he's a natural born leader, but like any young man he makes mistakes. He makes mistakes this second season, for sure.'

Despite the original mutterings of disapproval that Kit was too old to play the 14-year-old character from the book, he is now seen as a heartthrob, and many female fans are happy with the changes that Weiss and Benioff oversaw.

He found working on the second season harder than the first. 'It was harder because our outfits were bigger, that was the main difference,' he explained. 'Last year we were in the training yard with minimal stuff on, but here we're trekking north of the Wall and you've got your big cloak on, and then layers and layers of stuff – they just keep layering you up – and under that you have your thermals and so on. So when we were in Iceland, we choreographed a fight that we practised every day to where it got to a really sticky point.'

When they put on the costumes, it became even harder. 'And then we put on the costumes and we couldn't move. It was just like, this is useless, what are we going to do? But actually what it did is it informed the fight. Because in the real world, fights are dirty, vicious things; they're not eloquent and beautifully photographed. That's what we learned. It wasn't going to be beautiful to watch, it's not a flowing fight scene, it's going to be what it is: we're in a lot of gear, we're in that much snow – doing a fight in snow is something else – and it turned into a hard slog.'

Harington went on to explain that he'd gained more insight into his character as filming continued. 'I've really started to understand Jon more as we've gone on, and I think having a break between the first season and the second season,' he said. 'Weirdly, though I wasn't thinking about him every day, he matured in my head a bit. The first season, I loved doing, but I was always looking forward to the second. The first season was about his conflict, about whether he wants to be with his family or at the Wall, and he gets very inward. At the end of the first season, he finally makes the decision that he has his own war to fight. So the second season, it's very clear: he's determined, he's got a mission, he's going to do it. I thought that was an interesting shift for him.'

The actor was forced to cancel an appearance at July's Comic-Con panel in 2012 after he broke his ankle. HBO told the *Hollywood Reporter* that he did not injure himself on set and it would not interfere with the show's production.

JORAH MORMONT

Ser Jorah Mormont is a shamed and exiled knight who escaped execution after he was caught slave trading. It ruined an exemplary military career. He had received a knighthood for his bravery during the battle in Pyke to fight off the Greyjoy rebellion. Married once before (although little is known about this wife), Jorah met his second wife during the King's tourney to celebrate the victory. He fell in love with Lynesse Hightower instantly, asking, and being granted, her permission to wear her favour in the tournament. He fought off all comers to seal an unlikely win. That very night, he asked for her hand in marriage.

Lynesse came from a wealthy family, and grew miserable living on the isolated island where Mormont resided. Mormont subsequently drove himself to financial ruin trying to replicate her past glamorous life. To make money, he became a slave trader, breaking one of the Seven Kingdoms' oldest taboos.

Mormont's activities are discovered by Eddard Stark, and he is condemned to death. He flees to Lys with Lynesse and attempts to make a life as an exile. It isn't long, however, before Lynesse leaves him.

He becomes a mercenary, and eventually meets Viserys Targaryen and is taken into his service at the wedding of Daenerys. He begins to secretly report to Varys in the hope than he can finally receive a royal pardon. However, while he begins to greatly admire Daenerys, he has little time for Viserys – as is proved when he watches him be killed by Drogo. He shows more compassion for Daenerys, and, when he discovers there is a threat on her life from Varys, he steps in at just the right time to prevent her being killed.

Mormont guides the scared young lady and oversees her journey from one of doubt and nerves to that of strength, honour and power. He fights a Dothraki warrior to the death in order to protect her, and he is devastated when he believes she is to commit suicide to be reunited with her dead husband. However, he is shocked not only when she burns alive, but also when she survives, along with her hatched dragon eggs.

When they finally reach the city of Qarth, he ceases communication with the Seven Kingdoms. Another attempt is made on Daenerys' life by an assassin, but this time it's not Mormont who saves her life but a stranger called Arstan Whitebeard – who eventually turns out to be Barristan Selmy – the former Kingsguard who was stripped of his title when Joffrey was crowned King.

SPOILER

Selmy informs Daenerys that her right-hand man is actually an informer for Varys. At this point, Mormont has finally declared his love to Daenerys, and she has begun to grow tired of his advances. Shocked by the duplicitous nature of both men, she orders them to embark on a suicide mission. Both survive, however, and when Selmy begs for forgiveness she grants it.

Mormont, on the other hand, is less keen to do so, believing he has already shown his faith and loyalty to her. Displeased by his actions, she orders him to leave, and tells him that she will kill him if she sees him again.

Heading to Volantis, he spies Tyrion Lannister in a brothel – and he captures him in a bid to win back favour from Daenerys. However, their ship is attacked by slavers and they are sold as slaves, with Mormont forced to have a demon's face tattooed on his cheek. Someone tries to buy him, so they can chop off Mormont's head and give it to Daenerys as a wedding gift. Learning that she is getting married, he escapes from his new owner again and, along with Tyrion, joins the Sellsword company Second Sons.

Jorah Mormont is played with softly spoken charm by Iain Glen, an accomplished Scottish actor. Looking like a young Richard Chamberlain, he left the Royal Academy of Dramatic Art in 1985, and was acclaimed for his performance as imprisoned Scottish poet Larry Winters in *Silent Scream* (1990). He has successfully appeared on the small and big screen, as well on stage.

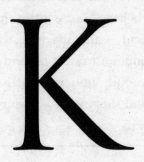

KINDLY MAN

SPOILER

The Kindly Man belongs to The Guild of the Faceless Men – a secret society of assassins who pray to the god of death, their Many-Faced God.

When Arya heads to Braavos to learn the Faceless Men's ways, the Kindly Man takes charge of her training. He first appears to Arya as a grotesque being, with a worm coming out of his eyehole. But, when Arya is summoned to bite the worm, the Kindly Man's face changes to that of a sweet old man.

When he believes she is ready, he gives Arya her first assignment – and she is instructed to kill the target only, and not to hurt his bodyguards. She does this by ingeniously noticing that he always bites his gold coins, and slipping in a poisoned one when he is not looking.

LITTLEFINGER

First seen as the Master of Coin on the King's Small Council, Lord Petyr Baelish, aka Littlefinger, is someone who claims to be sitting on the fence but, in fact, weaves an intricate web of lies and deceit. He devises cunning ploys and moves oblivious pawns to their death as he plays his own game of chess in a bid to win the biggest prize of all – power.

To come this far is something of a minor miracle for Littlefinger, who has spent many years attempting to better his lowly birthright. His father was an almost insignificant lord of an insignificant area near the Narrow Sea that sits between Westeros and the eastern continent of Essos.

After Hoster Tully struck up a friendship with Littlefinger's father, Littlefinger was sent to Riverrun castle as a foster child to be raised alongside the Lord Tully's children – Catelyn, Lysa and Edmure. He would eventually fall in love with Catelyn, but she would love him only as a brother.

After the announcement of the betrothal between Catelyn and Brandon Stark, Littlefinger unwisely challenges Brandon to a duel for her hand – a challenge that sees Littlefinger left with a huge scar on his chest, but alive to fight another day thanks to Catelyn, who tells Brandon to spare his life. Despite this, she does not speak to him afterwards, and even burns the letter that he sends after Brandon's death.

He also had problems with another of Tully's children – drunkenly bedding Catelyn's sister and impregnating her. However, Hoster Tully demanded that Lysa drink moon tea to abort the child because Littlefinger's family has such a lowly status.

He was banished from the Riverrun family, but Lysa continues a relationship with him, and, when she marries Lord Jon Arryn, the Hand to King Robert, she manages to ensure Littlefinger a customs job at the port city Gulltown.

Having impressed many people with his considerable finance skills, he is named Master of Coin in King's Landing, and he buys many brothels in the area.

SPOILER

It was discovered that Littlefinger manipulated Lysa to poison her husband after he found out that he was set to tell the King that his children weren't his and that, in fact, his wife's brother had fathered them. Lysa was led to believe her husband was sending her young son away to be fostered, and so she murdered him. She was further manipulated by Littlefinger, who convinced her to write a letter to her sister claiming that the Lannisters were involved in Jon's death. It's this letter that sends Ned Stark to King's Landing, and sparks a chain of events at the beginning of the series leading to the death of King Robert and the war that engulfs the Seven Kingdoms. He is also the one that leads Ned Stark to his death, after betraying him following King Robert's death.

Littlefinger thwarts a plot to whisk Sansa Stark away from King's Landing by informing Tywin of the plan. The elder Lannister then weds her to Tyrion to keep her there.

Because of his newfound status as a High Lord due to his work during the beginning of Joffrey's reign, Littlefinger is assigned to woo and marry Lysa Tully in an attempt to win over the neutral Vale of Arryn. Given his romantic dalliances with Lysa in the past,

Littlefinger sees it as an easy task. However, he stays close to King's Landing, having plotted the death of Joffrey. Sansa is taken to him following the King's death from a poison called The Strangler, and informs him that she is free from the Lannisters. He dyes her hair and she takes on a new identity – that of his bastard daughter Alayne Stone.

Littlefinger ends up marrying Lysa, but she grows jealous of his affection towards Sansa/Alayne and tries to kill her. However, Littlefinger stops Lysa, and after an argument he tells her he has only loved one woman, her sister Catelyn. He then shoves her out of the Moon Door and pins the blame on Marillion the singer.

He reveals to Sansa that the Seven Kingdoms is coming to ruin faster than he could have thought thanks to Cersei's doomed leadership at King's Landing.

In 2009, Aidan Gillen was told by a journalist that he appeared in two of the most iconic shows ever made – *Queer as Folk* and *The Wire*. 'Well, I did go out of my way to find those sorts of parts and those sorts of series,' he said. 'And for me that is still a mandate.'

And he added a third to his CV, after it was announced in 2010 that he was cast as Lord Petyr Baelish, or Littlefinger.

His name had been mentioned several times to play the slippery character and the casting news was met with joy by fans of the books.

Gillen noted, 'I did audition for it, as I do for probably about 50 per cent or maybe less of the things I end up doing. I'm not very good at auditions, but, if there's something I really want like *Game of Thrones*, that I may not necessarily be top of the list for, I'll do what I can to convince them to cast me. I wasn't really aware of the fan favourite thing, although someone did point it out to me after I'd been cast. So if that had any influence, and I know producers now actually, particularly on a project like that, do listen to the fans, thanks for that.'

Gillen first came to attention with his breakthrough role as the charismatic Stuart in the UK version of *Queer as Folk*, before starring in HBO's *The Wire* as plucky political schemer Mayor Carcetti.

'It seems to me that most characters, in anything, are flawed in some way, just like most people,' he said. 'You look for the good in the flawed people and vice versa, and then try and make them appealing in some way. It's always more interesting to take on someone that's going to have hidden sides or a fatal flaw, because there's going to be more to play with – more conflict, internally or in and around them – but it's probably the thing of finding the positive in there.

'I like the wide scope of the show, that there are so many strands in play – I like that it's tough, sad and funny. And that it's all rooted in real human experience with something like magic now starting to filter in. It's been earned and so can be believed.'

Speaking before the start of series two, he revealed, 'I'm actually trying to get out of playing villains now – maybe signing up for six seasons as Littlefinger goes against that, but I don't see him as a villain, more a brilliant strategist and survivor in a cut-throat world. There's some strong new characters, Robert's brother, Stannis, being a very obvious one to note. We see Littlefinger branch out and go on some travels, too, and it's nice to get out of the house. I have some dealings with Tyrion – he's really dominating the scene in King's Landing now. There's always a lot going on and there's no rush to pair everyone up with everyone. Having worked on *The Wire*, I know the merits of playing the long game. It's more interesting, not patronising.'

Costume designer Michele Clapton said about his costume, 'It's also interesting to look at Littlefinger's journey; he started off very much as a courtier, he was always very organised with his little chain and his notebook, and then suddenly he actually stopped wearing the mantle. He had just little glimpses of turquoise beneath his costume and the slit was cut slightly higher. Slowly you realise he ran brothels. His costumes, just slowly, became a little richer.'

LOCATIONS

Rugged lands and squalid harbours in an ancient medieval world; sunnier, majestic climates and a freezing landscape masquerading as the country Beyond the Wall were just some of the locations needed to bring Martin's written world to life. Weiss and Benioff faced a puzzling task in how to pull this off.

There were two options. They could film it in a studio with set backdrops masquerading as different lands, which would be a cheaper alternative but would look exactly that – cheap. The world that Martin created was lavished with so much detail it needed to feel real, which meant they had to go for option two – the filming would need to be done in several locations around the world, posing a headache for HBO as they attempted to keep control of a production that would be split around the globe.

In 2009, it was confirmed that the series would be shot in Northern Ireland, with the area's First Minister Peter Robinson, announcing, 'This is the first time that a TV production of such vast size and scale has been filmed in Northern Ireland. The announcement comes following the visit by the Deputy First Minister and I to Los Angeles in March. It will be a welcome boost to the production sector, helping develop the industry here and bringing employment and investment to Northern Ireland. HBO is a recognised worldwide brand, with their programmes broadcast in over 150 countries. Securing this project over a number of competitors is a major coup for Northern Ireland. HBO has an enviable reputation for offering very high-quality, original programming, receiving critical acclaim for its productions, including *Sex and the City*, *Six Feet Under*, *Band of Brothers* and, of course, *The Sopranos*.'

The main filming for seasons one and two took place at the Paint Hall Studios in Belfast. They also exploited the rugged scenery of Ireland to double for the many scenes in the North and other locations around Westeros.

'We've been able to find an incredible variety of locations,' Frank Doelger, one of the executive producers of the series, told UTV. 'The weather is definitely a challenge, but I have to let you know that we've been rained out in Malta, we've been rained out in Croatia, we've been snowed out in Iceland. So all the other areas that we've gone to have been challenging as well.'

Sandy Brae, in the Mourne Mountains, stood in for Vaes Dothrak, a city where the Dothraki enter. County Down's Castle Ward was used for the courtyard scenes of Ned Stark's ancestral home, and is the location for the first meeting we see between King Robert and Ned and his family. Saintfield Estates also doubles up as Winterfell's godswood. Tollymore Forest was used extensively in the first part of the pilot, with the dead children, and when Ned finds the direwolves. Cairncastle in County Antrim is where Ned beheads the deserter. In season two, they needed to find a location for the Iron Islands – home to the seafaring Greyjoys – and they chose Lordsport Harbour.

The show's location manager, Robert Boake, said, 'Because our story reached out toward seagoing adventures and featured the Iron Islands and Pyke, [we] needed something brand new and spectacular.'

Malta's Mdina doubled up for the King's Landing – the capital city of the Seven Kingdoms. The huge medieval city stands impressive on a hill but is an inland city, which is not how it is described in the books, and they were limited to interior shots such as side streets.

Fort Manoel nearby doubled up as the Great Sept of Baelor. Island of Gozo's The Azure Window was used for Daenerys Targaryen's wedding to Khal Drogo.

Shooting in Malta lasted six weeks, but was marred because of an environmental fiasco when construction sand was thrown over the rocks at Gozo's Dwejra – with the local production company fined €86,500 and ordered to pay the cost of cleaning up the mess.

King's Landing and the Red Keep moved to Croatia in season two to capitalise on, according to Weiss, a 'full-on, immaculately preserved medieval walled city that actually looks uncannily like King's Landing'.

'That was in and of itself such an amazing find,' Weiss stated, with Benioff adding, 'King's Landing might be the single most important location in the entire show, and it has to look right.'

The Island of Lokrum just off the coast of Dubrovnik doubled for the City of Qarth, with a set built at the Dubac quarry for the gates of the city that Daenerys visits in season two.

Filming in Croatia began in September 2011, and the Maltese officials understandably sought answers for the production team's decision to move. HBO moved fast to explain the switch had nothing to do with the Dwejra sand saga, saying, 'We are shooting different scenes for the second series and Croatia was able to offer us the look we needed for those additional locations.'

The Malta Film Commission said, 'We were pursuing that line of thought and trying to contact the production to find out why it did not return to Malta. Once a production chooses Malta, 50 per cent of the job is done but the other half is proving it was the right choice. No repeat business does not necessarily translate into a bad experience but we would still have questioned why the production did not come back.'

With season two showing more of the dangers that lie Beyond the Wall, they chose Iceland to replicate the savage land that is the home of the wildings and White Walkers –

with the Svinafellsjokull calving glacier in Skaftafell bearing the brunt of filming, followed by shooting near Smyrlabjorg and Vik on Hofdabrekkuheidi.

Line producer Chris Newman said, 'In season one, we had places we could snow up with artificial snow, but north of the Wall in season two when Jon Snow goes to the Frostfangs demanded a bigger landscape.'

'We always knew we wanted something shatteringly beautiful and barren and brutal for this part of Jon's journey, because he's in the true North now,' added Benioff. 'It's all real. It's all in camera. We're not doing anything in postproduction to add mountains or snow or anything.'

Kit Harington said about filming in Iceland, a place he visited when he was younger, 'I swore I'd go back. It's one of those places that I went to as a teenager and all I really wanted to do was chase skirt, but it shocked us how beautiful it was. We spent the whole time gawking at the landscapes.

'It's like landing on the moon. It's like landing on an alien landscape. There's no trees; it's very barren. That's the first thing you reckon with – it feels very moon-like. It's strange. It's a country of extremes. It's got these huge glaciers sticking out of very flat lands. It's stunning to behold, definitely.'

There was a setback to filming in Croatia in series three,

with concern over securing the funds from the Croatian that would enable HBO to film there. However, everything fell into place, and filming in Croatia went ahead.

MAD KING

While the latter parts of his reign would see him dubbed the Mad King, or Aerys the Mad, he was known as Aerys II Targaryen – the 17th and final member of the Targaryen dynasty to sit upon the Iron Throne.

His initial reign saw great promise, making sweeping changes to the court at King's Landing. He felt it had been filled with stuffy old men, and needed more youth and vigour – and appointed the young ruthless Lord Tywin Lannister as the King's Hand.

It was a peaceful reign for 12 years, but things began to sour after the King heard rumours that Tywin had boasted that he was really the King. Aerys began to distance himself from his Hand, solving more problems by himself, and he even rejects a Tywin's proposal that his daughter Cersei should marry Aerys' son, Rhaegar.

Aerys was abducted and held prisoner for several months by a rebellious lord, and after his release he was never the same again – and his paranoia and insanity began to grow. After the abduction, he distrusted Tywin, Rhaegar and his wife, and appointed Lord Varys as Master of Whispers after hearing about his talents.

He also developed a huge obsession with the incredibly flammable substance wildfire, stocking huge amounts and eventually burying them beneath the city with the plan to destroy King's Landing if his reign was to come to an end.

Aerys was becoming a harsh and cruel King, dishing out vindictive punishments, including burning Ned Stark's dad alive, and concocting a device that saw Ned's brother Brandon be strangled the more he struggled and tried to free his father.

It was this chain of events that led to King Robert's Rebellion, which would eventually overthrow the Mad King. Fearing his time was coming to an end, Aerys tried to unleash his plan to destroy the city, but before he could he was killed by Jaime Lannister. According to Jaime, the Mad King feared he would survive the fire and be brought back as a dragon.

MANCE RAYDER

The man dubbed the King-Beyond-the-Wall, Mance Rayder is a lean man, who turned his back on his duties as a member of the Night's Watch to join the wildings, teaching them new manoeuvres and shaping them into a formidable fighting team.

He was born a wilding before he was taken by the Night's Watch as a child and raised among them at Castle Black. He is a loyal member, until he is healed by a female wilding after suffering an injury during a ranging mission. She looks after him and even mends his cloak with new fabric. However, upon his return to the Wall, he is stunned when they order him to replace his mended uniform. Wishing for a life where he could make more of his own choices, he abandons his oath and the life he knew to live with the wildings.

Rayder is discussed many times during the first two seasons of *Game of Thrones*, and is eventually revealed to the viewer during the third season.

SPOILER

Jon Snow has gone undercover from the Night's Watch in a bid to infiltrate Rayder's army. However, Snow discovers that they are living in fear of the evil things that plague the vast lands, and they want to take over the Wall merely to defend themselves against the creatures.

Rayder attempts to invade the Wall, but Snow and a skeleton crew of the Night's Watch men somehow manage to hold them off until Stannis gets there. Stannis orders Rayder to be burned alive, but his fire sorceress Melisandre spares him by using a spell to make another man look like him.

Rayder is currently being held captive by Ramsay Bolton and has sewed together skins in a cage to keep himself warm.

NED STARK

One of the key aspects in George R. R. Martin's world is the notion that no one is safe. It's something that is evidenced time and time again. This is a dangerous world, and, while there are heroes, they are not of the superhuman kind. They make mistakes, they bleed and they will die – some quicker than others.

The death of Lord Eddard 'Ned' Stark was the signal that this was not the sort of show you normally expect. The seemingly 'lead' characters don't die only towards the end of a series either – certainly not in the case of Ned anyway.

Martin pulls the rug wonderfully from under your feet

because he knows people's expectations of heroes, and he throws people off the scent even more as he signals an intent to free Stark from the Lannisters' capture if he admits a betrayal to the throne. It goes against everything this honourable man stands for, but it allows him to ensure his children's safety. It seems an appropriate punishment – wound the leading man but don't kill him. The expectation is that he will go home an emotionally hurt man, but will come back to fix his pride at a later date with revenge against the Lannisters. But that is not how it goes.

The character, who was at the forefront of the advertising campaign, simply dies, beheaded in front of a baying crowd. It's a dynamic scene, and is reminiscent of the death that Janet Leigh suffered in *Psycho*. She was a big star at the time, and the whole film was geared towards her character as she escapes from a town with stolen money. Instead, she is merely a victim of Norman Bates fairly early on, and it's only then that we realise the film only really starts when she is killed. The same happens in *Game of Thrones*: the whole series kicks off the moment Ned dies. Suddenly, houses go to war against each other, murmurs of discontent sweep the Seven Kingdoms and a number of people attempt to seize the Iron Throne for themselves.

The website *winteriscoming.net* wrote the following after the screen death aired on TV: 'Most of us knew this was coming, but for many that knowledge didn't make Ned's

Above: George R. R. Martin. The man behind the complex fantasy novels and TV series *Game of Thrones*.

Below: A stellar cast was picked for the first series, including Sean Bean. *From left*: Nikolaj Coster-Waldau (Jamie Lannister), Emilia Clarke (Daenerys Targaryen), Sean Bean (Eddard Stark) and Mark Addy (Robert Baratheon).

Kit Harington plays the complex character Jon Snow, Eddard Stark's bastard son, who is sworn to the Night's Watch in season one.

The Lannister family is one of seven noble families fighting for the control of Westeros.

Above left: Nikolaj Coster-Waldau plays the 'King Slayer', Jamie Lannister, brother to Cersei and Tyrion, and son of Tywin.

Above right: Peter Dinklage was perfectly cast to play the role of Tyrion Lannister, a popular character who is equally cunning as he is humorous.

Below left: Charles Dance plays Tywin Lannister.

Below right: The role of Cersei Lannister, a hard-faced and power crazy queen, is well played out by the talented Lena Headey.

The role of Daenerys
Targaryen was given to
the beautiful and young
actress Emilia Clarke.

Aidan Gillen was already a well-established actor before taking on the role of manipulative Petyr 'Littlefinger' Baelish.

Gwendoline Christie was chosen to play the loyal character Brienne of Tarth.

From left: Alfie Allen (Theon Greyjoy), Gethin Anthony (Renly Baratheon), Finn Jones (Ser Loras Tyrell) and Kit Harington (Jon Snow) enjoying some downtime.

The Stark family – fighting to keep Winterfell, reunite their family and crown Robb Stark the official King of the North.

Above left: Isaac Hempstead Wright plays the young cripple Bran Stark.

Above right: Irish-born Michelle Fairley portrays the loyal and wise Catelyn Stark, mother to Robb, Bran, Sansa, Arya and Rickon.

Below left: Maisie Williams (Arya) *left* and Sophie Turner (Sansa) *right* at a *Game of Thrones* press night.

Below right: British actor Richard Madden plays the role of Robb Stark.

death any easier. For fans of George R. R. Martin's *A Song of Ice and Fire*, this was the seminal moment. The death of Eddard Stark was a wakeup call to every person holding that book in their hands: no matter what you were used to, no matter what came before, no matter how certain you were in the tropes and the traditions of fantasy writing – this was when you sat up, eyes wide. This put fear into you. If this guy could die.'

Executive producer Weiss commented, 'Ned dying is telling a hard truth about the price of honour and the price of morality in a world where not everybody has the same values as you do. It's not a simplistic redemptive message, where you sacrifice yourself and it saves the day. A lot of times sacrifice ends up being futile.'

Still, while it was written in the book, it's another thing for a TV series to hire a big star, promote the show with his star status and then kill him before the first season has even ended.

However, HBO is a different beast to most TV networks, and, while Weiss and Benioff had hundreds, if not thousands, of meetings with their bosses over how to adapt this series, there was never any murmur of discontent about the death of Ned Stark.

He was played by Sean Bean, a big star thanks to roles in *The Lord of the Rings* movies and *Patriot Games*, and as the Bond villain in 1995's *GoldenEye*. Despite a career playing mainly bad guys, Bean rose to fame as the maverick Napoleonic Wars rifleman Richard Sharpe in the hit British series *Sharpe*. The roguish officer stole the hearts of female viewers, with the male ones impressed by his rousing derring-do. So who better to play the noble Lord in *Game of Thrones*.

Martin announced on his blog in 2009: 'For the movie fans out there, Sean Bean needs no introduction. I mean, what the hell, he was Boromir (in *Lord of the Rings*) and he was Sharpe, he was terrific in both roles, and in a hundred other parts besides. I can't imagine a better Ned. The deal took some doing, so my fingers have been crossed for a month now (and boy, that made it hard to type), but now it's done, and I'm thrilled.'

'It's a good thing to be typecast, isn't it?' Bean said to *Collider* about playing another fantasy character. 'I suppose it's similar to *The Lord of the Rings* in its size, its quality, its magic and its danger. I happen to enjoy playing the kind of roles with riding horses, swinging swords, having fights, wearing wigs and growing beards, even though I don't first thing in the morning, when it takes you about three hours to get ready. I do have affinity to that kind of role. I think the good thing about *Game of Thrones* is that there is such score for it. *The Lord of the Rings* was three films, and they thoroughly researched it, and it was very well replicated on screen. But, with what George has created, it's a very different world. It goes on much, much further and much longer, and there's many more twists and turns, but I certainly enjoy this genre.'

And he was delighted when he first met David and Dan. 'I read the book and found it very exciting, very luxuriant, very dangerous, very edgy and very sexy. That's very flattering. I'm very flattered that I was chosen to play this part.'

News of his casting met with near-universal endorsement, with Bean adding, 'I'm not really familiar with computers and blog sites and stuff like that, but I've heard some good things. So that's encouraging. They seem to think I'm a suitable choice for the role so I'm flattered by that.'

And talking about his death, he said, 'It's quite heroic, I suppose. I didn't just get knocked off and nobody notices. Plenty of people noticed. It was a good one. It really sets the standard, which is high already, for what you would expect from HBO. This was a courageous venture to take on in the first place, with such a vast, big-scale production, and this very bold, daring narrative structure. It's a good thing about George R. R. He's prepared to kill off the main guys. You don't get the feeling that the good guy is going to last forever, like James Bond.'

Bean admitted, 'He's such a predominant character, straight through all of it, and you think, "Wait a minute, what's happening?" He's obviously been betrayed left and right and centre, but you never thought it would come to this. Even the shock on his face before it happens, it's like, "But we made a deal." It's a pretty awful ending and the kids are watching as well.'

'We were in Malta in the middle of a big square,' he added. 'A big piazza with hundreds and hundreds of people on a raised platform. I'm making a last speech; I have my hands tied behind my back. I kind of say that I have betrayed the realm and I have been a traitor in order to save my children. It's real heartbreaking stuff.'

NIGHT'S WATCH

The military order that is the Night's Watch gives those that are underprivileged, not born to royalty or far down the line for a place on the throne a chance to seize some glory of their own. With luck, bravery and dedication, it's entirely feasible for these lost men to find themselves in a position of power and be looked upon with high regard at the stronghold of Castle Black.

Of course, there are obvious disadvantages. Their job is to guard the imposing and immense fortification known as the Wall, which keeps out the wildings and a number of unspecified creatures that haunt their nightmares. Some believe their tales from childhood of things that go bump in the dark from Beyond the Wall, while some disregard them as nonsensical fairytales.

The latter opinion has become the norm when the series begins. The Night's Watch is less honoured than before, with numbers dwindling, and new members that swear the oath not loyal soldiers but former prisoners and thieves faced with an ultimatum of being maimed or spending their lives guarding the Wall.

Those that swear the oath must live a life of celibacy, and can never desert their brothers. Punishment for deserting is death by beheading, as witnessed in one of the early scenes of the first episode.

There are three groups within the Watch: the Stewards, who look after the needs of the members of the Watch, the Builders, who maintain the stronghold and the Wall, and the Rangers, who patrol the dark forest.

The wall, which is a staggering 700ft high, separates the Seven Kingdoms from the North. Jeor Mormont is the Lord Commander of the Night's Watch – a gruff but honourable man, who believes change is coming from the North and fears for the lives of his men. He is held in great esteem by his men, and is always accompanied by a raven.

Mormont marched to war with Lord Stark during Robert's Rebellion, before joining the Night's Watch six years later, and rapidly moving through the ranks to become Lord Commander.

As Lord of Bear Island, Jeor marched to war under Lord Eddard Stark's banner during Robert's Rebellion. Concerned by the dwindling numbers, he used it to his advantage, dropping the regular patrols for a more random system so wildings could never guess when they would happen.

Mormont is played by veteran Scottish actor James Cosmo, who said of the series in 2011, 'It's pretty violent, and pretty sexy, with lots of political intrigue. They conjure up a wonderful world. It's got a *Lord of the Rings* mythical quality to it, but there's horror elements and zombies, and lots of swords and horses.'

One of the recruiters for the Wall is Yoren, a man who joined the order after killing his brother's murderer with an axe. Yoren, played by former *EastEnders* actor Francis Magee, travels around the Seven Kingdoms, usually to castle jails, recruiting new members. During the first season, Tyrion Lannister takes a liking to Yoren, and they both head off to King's Landing. Their journey together ends when Tyrion is captured by Catelyn Stark and men dedicated to the Starks, but Yoren flees to the Red Keep where he tells Ned Stark about his wife's actions.

It's Yoren who grabs Arya in the square following her father's execution, and quickly cuts her hair and instructs her to pose as a boy to avoid detection from the Lannisters. He is killed by royal soldiers after refusing to surrender a recruit.

The greatest daily threat to the Night's Watch are the wildings, or the Free Folk as they are known. Groups regularly cross over the Wall on raiding trips. They are seen as nothing but a nuisance by some, but are becoming an organised and deadly unit under the leadership of the former Night's Watch member with the self-imposed tag of King-Beyond-the-Wall, Mance Rayder. The charismatic leader plots an invasion against the Seven Kingdoms to escape the threat from the Others. The Others are creatures that roam the sparse lands Beyond the Wall.

Kit Harington, who plays Jon Snow, a member of the Night's Watch, said of the Watch to the *Huffington Post*, 'In Jon's head, he is very loyal to the Night's Watch. To forsake his family, his brothers and sisters down South and after all that's happened in the first season, his position now lies with the Night's Watch. He has to be 100 per cent loyal to them because if it was anything less, he would have gone South. I think in Jon's head – and this is where I've had to piece it together myself as to what his future plans are – I think he does want to avenge his father. He does want to join his brother eventually, and he wants to tie his position in the Night's Watch into being able to do those things, to take his revenge on Joffrey. How he's going to do that, I don't think he knows yet, but he's adamant that he will, sometime in the future. His main priority at the moment has to be with his commander and his mission North of the Wall. He hides from everyone, but he has a burning ambition to go South and to join his brother's war, but he can't do that yet.'

ORIGINAL PILOT

When news of the cast was announced, a quick glance at the many forums, message boards and comment sections underneath the stories saw just how excited – if slightly bemused – the fans were about it. 'This is really happening, isn't it?' wrote one, an opinion that echoed sentiments all over the internet.

In October 2009, the unthinkable had happened – the unfilmable novel was being filmed. Lasting nearly a month, the pilot was shot in Northern Ireland, Scotland and Morocco.

When a show interests a TV network, they usually

commission a pilot episode just to see exactly what they will be getting. A script and excited producers can only go so far; until they see it with their own eyes, there will always be a touch of scepticism and hands wrapped around the budget.

It's rare that a series will be commissioned without a pilot first, and it's unlikely that, even if it gets a series commission, the pilot that is shown to executives will be exactly the same as the one that makes it to the viewers.

Executives scrawl notes and demands, and changes often happen. A cast member can be replaced, whether it's because it didn't work out or, as is the usual case, their schedules make it impossible. It's one thing to clear space in your diary for a month, but, as it can take up to a year for executives to finally agree on whether a show gets the go ahead, it's unfair to point fingers at those who agree to another job while waiting for the series to finally get the green light. That is certainly what happened with *Game of Thrones*.

The original pilot was directed by *The Wire* actor Thomas McCarthy. He had impressed with his indie film *Station Agent*, which starred Peter Dinklage. Weiss and Benioff were delighted to land him, but, when they came to reshoot the pilot, he ended up making indie wrestling film *Win Win*, and was replaced by Tim Van Patten.

'I did a lot of the casting,' McCarthy said to

AVCLUB.com. 'I think we did some good work. But they've had to reshoot and rethink so much of it since I left, and I've had no involvement in that because of *Win Win*. I finished that right before Thanksgiving and went into *Win Win* over the holiday, so I literally had a week or two of downtime. I turned in an early cut, and they had to recast, and I think they rethought. You know, they're taking on this huge book, and they rethought how to get into it and how to set it up. They had to change some locations, and they did quite a bit of work on it since I left. I'd like to think I had some impact on it, but I don't think much of that is mine anymore.'

Benioff spoke about McCarthy to *bullz-eye.com* while making the original pilot, 'Well, Tom's really smart, for one thing, so talking to him about the project got us excited about his vision for it, and I loved his movies. I think we both loved his movies and the way he works with actors. And, you know, the feeling was the other way to go was potentially to get someone who was known for doing the big effects things and the lavish spectacles, and, for us, what made this story we weren't going to try to compete with Peter Jackson and *Lord of the Rings*. There's no way we could. What we could do with this story, though, is spend a lot of time with these characters − they're wonderful characters − and really get to know them and get incredibly in-depth and incredibly intimate.'

Benioff and Weiss both felt this was something Tom did better than most directors. 'And, you know, the last couple of movies, I think of Peter Dinklage's character, for instance, in *The Station Agent*, and just how much I loved that character,' Benioff continued. 'I wanted to spend more time with that character and was upset when the movie ended, and I felt like Tom could really bring that kind of direction to the actors and begin this journey for them.

'It was really educational for us to watch how he handled the casting process and how he, as an actor, had been through this drill I can only imagine dozens, probably hundreds of times, just gave him an empathy for the person sitting there. Because casting can be, I would imagine, a very uncomfortable experience for an actor, but he really made people feel at home, and when they walked into that room, it didn't matter if they were great or they were not so great, nobody left there feeling bad. That's a very cool thing.'

Some of his scenes remained in the shown pilot, and, because he helped with the casting, McCarthy received a Consulting Producer credit.

McCarthy said, 'The guy [Van Patten] who did the second episode, when they were doing all the reshoots, he took on the first. I couldn't do it. And I just didn't feel connected to it. It wasn't a big decision. It felt right. It felt like more of it was his than mine in terms of what you see on the screen now, and I think if you would talk to them, they would say I was helpful in a lot of the process, but it certainly doesn't feel like mine. It's really not a director's medium. I think there are some really good TV directors, but that is a writers' medium and a studio's medium. There was a good learning curve on that, but I don't think it's anything I'll rush back to.'

As well as different actresses playing Catelyn Stark and Daenerys Targaryen in the original pilot, the brief role of Waymar Royce was originally played by *Harry Potter* star Jamie Campbell Bower. Roger Allam played Illyrio Mopatis in the series, but Ian McNeice played him in the pilot, with Dermot Keaney replacing Richard Ridings for the part of Gared.

Roy Dotrice was cast as Grand Maester Pycelle, but his scene was cut from the pilot. However, producers still wanted him, but he fell ill and was replaced by *Star Wars: Episode V* and *Indiana Jones and the Last Crusade* actor Julian Glover.

Doune Castle in Scotland was used to stand in for Winterfell, with the Daenerys and Dothraki scenes being shot in Morocco rather than Malta as in the series.

Author George R. R. Martin filmed a cameo at Daenerys' wedding, but the scene was excised from the shoot. 'It was, sad to say, left on the cutting-room floor,' said Martin. 'It was during Daenerys' wedding and I was a Pentoshi nobleman in the background, wearing a gigantic hat.'

Martin has previously mooted the idea of appearing in the show, telling *Empire*, 'I also had investigated the idea of being a head on a spike, and David and Dan were going to put my severed head on a spike at one point, but then they got the quote for what that would cost. Those severed heads are expensive and our budget is tight! So unless I provide my own I don't get to be a severed head! But one of my fans who does that sort of thing has offered me the chance to make one next time I go out to LA. How could I resist? I could have my own severed head and carry it around in a bowling bag.'

Other scenes that made into the final aired series include King Robert and Eddard Stark's conversation in the Winterfell crypts, and Ned and his brother's conversation about the dead ranger.

HBO programming chief Michael Lombardo was thrilled when he saw early footage, calling it 'fantastic' and said executives were 'on pins and needles' while they waited for the rough cut. 'The director got great performances,' he said. 'Unlike a lot of projects like this, everything was shot on location. It has such a rich texture that it looks more expensive than it actually was. The fantasy is so incidental; it has a very adult tone. You forget it's fantasy while you're watching it, and that's what I love about it. I would be surprised if it doesn't [get the green light]. It has everything going for it.'

Benioff told *Collider*, 'It was a good experience for us, in that we got to go back and do much of the pilot over again and learn from some of the mistakes we made the first time, some of which were scripted ones. You take certain things for granted, from reading the books. You think certain relationships are clear. We would show the original pilot to friends of ours, who are very intelligent friends that watch very carefully, and they would get to the end of the pilot and have no idea that Cersei Lannister and Jaime Lannister were brother and sister, which grew into the last scene of the show. So, we clarified some of the relationships. We also had shot the Dothraki wedding scenes in Morocco originally, which made a certain amount of sense, practically and budgetarily. We had great sets that we could use there, which had been built for *Kingdom of Heaven* for Ridley Scott. But Malta ultimately made a lot more sense for a location than Morocco had. And there were a couple of recasting moves, which had been made, that necessitated reshooting all the scenes.'

McCarthy added to *AVCLUB.com*, 'I think the great shows, *The Wire*, *Sopranos*, *Six Feet Under* – I think there was a very clear understanding of whose show it was, and I think those guys who made those shows, there was a singular vision there. I think that show can get there; I just think it was hard for me, not being so involved. I finished it and walked away, and I've never done that with anything. I'm a perfectionist and I like to be involved. I liked a lot of the people I worked with; I worked with some really talented people on that project. But it felt a little more like a job.'

PETER DINKLAGE

Peter Dinklage is the only male actor to get his own chapter in this book, but, as anyone who has seen his performance as the roguish Tyrion will know, if anyone deserves more focus it's Dinklage.

When news of the show was announced, one of the first questions asked was who would play Tyrion the Imp. It was actually a question that the show's bosses and Martin had pondered very briefly – with Dinklage their only choice to play the much-loved dwarf.

'When I read George's books,' Benioff said, 'I decided Tyrion Lannister was one of the great characters in literature.

Not just fantasy literature – literature. A brilliant caustic, horny, drunken, self-flagellating mess of a man. And there was only one choice to play him.'

There were certainly similarities. Obviously, they were roughly the same size (although Martin noted that Dinklage was almost too tall and handsome for the character as described in his books), but they also had the same attitude.

Dinklage said to *Rolling Stone*, 'When you're reminded so much of who you are by people – not a fame thing, but with my size, constantly, growing up – you either curl up in a corner in the dark or you wear it proudly, like armour or something. You can turn it on its head and use it before anybody else gets a chance.'

He was born with achondroplasia in 1969 in New Jersey to his music-teacher mother and his insurance-salesman father. Being a dwarf wasn't something that was registered in Dinklage's household ('I think I would have remembered it, or it would have stood out'), with nothing moved from the high shelves to aid him. If he wanted it, he would have to find a way to reach it.

Inspired by The Who albums, he would put on puppet rock shows with his older brother for elderly people in his parents' basement. He would also perform to the song 'Send in the Clowns': 'I would dress in some sort of wig, but not dressed as a clown – I knew from an early age not to humiliate myself,' he revealed to *Rolling Stone* magazine. 'I was on a tricycle, and we played the entire song, and my whole part of the revue was to ride the tricycle and fall over, while these old people were sitting there. It's really a sad visual now that I think about it, a six-year-old little guy who keeps falling over on a tricycle. But if you ask any actor, they have those stories, they turn to that stuff. I don't know if Robert De Niro was doing puppet shows in his basement, but he was doing something.'

Growing up, he began to be more withdrawn, dressing in black and smoking cigarettes all day. 'When I was younger, definitely, I let it get to me. As an adolescent, I was bitter and angry, and I definitely put up these walls. But the older you get, you realise you just have to have a sense of humour. You just know that it's not your problem. It's theirs.'

However, drama became more of an outlet, and he has to thank a teacher for this, for making him showcase his talents in an Irish play called *Sharon's Grave*. 'It was the first time I played a part written for somebody my size,' Dinklage explained. 'He was just this wretched guy who was carried around on the back of his older, dim-witted brother, sort of an *Of Mice and Men* relationship. It was like, "Oh, wow there are things out there, it's not just Gilbert and Sullivan, there are these parts out there." It was only later that I ran away from roles that were specific to people my size.'

He studied drama at Bennington College – a period which he described thus: 'I smoked too much pot, stayed up too late, did a lot of plays, listened to a lot of Pixies and Dinosaur Jr.'

In 1995, he made his feature debut in the movie *Living in Oblivion*, playing a frustrated actor annoyed with the clichéd dwarf parts he gets. But, despite the performance, he still couldn't find an agent. 'I just wasn't a type that agents were looking for,' he said. 'I was too specific. They didn't have the imagination to send me on auditions for things that weren't written for a dwarf. They would only see ads at Christmas time, and if I didn't want to do those, what business would I bring them?'

Dinklage was thrust into the limelight for his role in the award-winning 2003 drama *The Station Agent*, which was directed by Thomas McCarthy, who helmed the original *Game of Thrones* pilot. It was a break-out role that would lead to him starring in both the UK and US version of *Death at a Funeral*, as well as *Elf* and *The Chronicles of Narnia: Prince Caspian* – a role in a fantasy drama that went against his usual choice.

He imagined what his teenage self would have thought of him wearing pointy shoes and a fake beard for the sequel to *The Lion, the Witch and the Wardrobe*:

'He would have given me shit, totally. But fuck him. "Go enjoy your mac-and-cheese again for dinner. Look under your oven – oh, yeah, that is a rat. I'm jet-setting first class, man. I'll see you later." That's what I'd say to that snob.'

However, he always attempted to avoid fantasy roles, given the stereotype connotations. 'I always wonder, "Why are all these fantasy books, especially for children, fascinated with people my size being fantastical creatures." Growing up, I was always like, "Really?" That was my big thing. Maybe Tolkien, or whoever, never met somebody my size. And if they did, maybe if they had been friends with somebody who was a dwarf they wouldn't have written it that way.'

However, he notes, there is a huge difference between other fantasy stories and *Game of Thrones*. 'That's what I liked about that show, he does have a sexual appetite,' he told *Rolling Stone* magazine. 'You never see one of those Narnian creatures with that.'

And Dinklage would also be a hit on the small screen – with credits including *Nip/Tuck*, *30 Rock* and *Entourage*.

In 2005, he married theatre director Erica Schmidt, and in 2011 their daughter was born. He moved from Manhattan to a more rural area of New York because of the fan attention. 'I can't be anonymous,' he said. His wife agreed:

'Even if they don't recognise him, they think he's Wee Man from *Jackass* or they think he's the guy from *In Bruges*.

Lena Headey said of Dinklage, who she has worked with twice, in a failed pilot in 2006 and in *Game of Thrones*, 'He truly is just who he is. There's nothing about him that isn't anything but confident.'

QARTH

The ancient port city Qarth is located on the Essos continent, and is a place of great wealth –with stunning architecture and grand furnishings.

It's a city full of spice traders and successful businessmen and it is the city in which Daenerys seeks shelter along with her withering band of followers.

It's also home to Warlocks, who are known as the Undying of Qarth. Despite their fearsome reputation, their powers have waned over the years, but that changes with the arrival of Daenerys and her dragons. They feel their powers growing stronger and they eventually capture the creatures and Daenerys, and place them in The House of the Undying Ones – also known as the Palace of Dust.

Few ever come out of there, but Daenerys successfully rescues her dragons, with the Undying all dead. The city is also known for the assassins known as the Sorrowful Men. These polite killers whisper sorry when they kill you.

RED WEDDING

'The scene that we cannot mention. I just remember reading the book before we'd even written the pilot and thinking, "Oh, my God, we've got to get this. We've got to get this show to happen because if we can make this scene work, it's gonna be one of the greatest things ever on television or film."'

Benioff wasn't joking. The Red Wedding is one, if not *the*, main talking point of the series; a devastating, heartrending scene that wrenches the gut and tears the heart.

The very first instalment of *A Song of Ice and Fire* showed that Martin's world is a violent one where no one is safe. The author was deliberate in that one, reasoning to *Entertainment Weekly*, 'It's really irritating when you open a book, and 10 pages into it you know that the hero you met on page one or two is gonna come through unscathed, because he's the hero. This is completely unreal, and I don't like it. If I was a soldier going to war, I'd be pretty scared the night before a battle. It's a scary thing.' Martin very much wanted his readers to feel that fear, as 'I want them to feel that no one is safe – that if my character is surrounded by three people with swords, he's in serious trouble, because he's only one guy against three. It's a great way to show that you're not writing this cartoon adventure where the hero is going to slay 20 men at once with his brilliant swordsmanship and go through unscathed while making wisecracks all the way.'

The death of Ned showed that the gloves were off in Westeros, and many other much-loved characters have suffered the same fate. However, none had the same impact, not even Ned Stark, as the bloodletting at the Red Wedding.

The events are documented in the third book, *A Storm of Swords*, with many expecting it to be the final event of series three, as the producers are splitting book three into two seasons – series three and series four.

SPOILER

When Catelyn Stark seals the deal with House Frey for her King in the North son, Robb, to gain an initiative in his war against the Lannisters, he is informed that one of the terms is a marriage pact between himself and Lord Walder Frey's daughter. It's a light moment in the series, with Robb resigned to the pact much to the amusement of his men.

However, it kick-starts a devastating chain of events that leads to the slaughter of Catelyn and himself, as well as most of his 3,500 bannermen.

Despite the marriage pact, when Lord Frey finds out Robb has wed behind his back, he begins plotting his revenge with Tywin Lannister.

As a peace offering, Catelyn and Robb are invited to the wedding of Edmure Tully and Lord Frey's daughter Roslin – an offer they can't decline after already causing offence to one of their allies.

The wedding is a raucous affair, but Robb is unaware that his bannermen are getting too drunk for what awaits them, and that the musicians are actually knights waiting to strike – and strike they do, butchering the North men. The rigged feast tents collapse and are then set on fire.

Wounded by arrows, Robb's life is finally ended

with a knife to the heart by Roose Bolton (played by Irish actor Michael McElhatton) The Freys cut off Robb's lifeless head and that of his direwolf, with the animal's head then stitched on to Robb's body as a mocking gesture about the slain King's relationship with the creature.

Lady Catelyn Stark's throat is slit and she is thrown naked into a river.

Martin wrote the scene last while working on the third book because he knew it would be heartrending to write. It was inspired by the young King of Scotland James II, who was beheaded after he was invited to a castle under the promise of safe conduct. '[It was] the hardest to write,' Martin said of the scene. 'That was the most violent and difficult. And I've gotten a lot of mail from readers, many of them saying it was brilliant, but others saying they couldn't read past that, and they were giving up on my book, it was too painful. But it's supposed to be painful. It was painful to write, it should be painful to read, it should be a scene that rips your heart out, and fills you with terror and grief. That's what I'm striving for.'

Martin told *Empire*, 'I have a huge emotional attachment to characters I've created, especially the viewpoint characters. When I'm writing from a character's viewpoint, in essence I become that character; I share their thoughts,

I see the world through their eyes and try to feel everything they feel. So when you share that bond with someone, even a fictional someone, it does become difficult to kill them. So that's why the Red Wedding was so painful – and there are other painful things too. So it is difficult to kill off a viewpoint character in particular. But on the other hand, I love creating new characters, as you can tell by the number that I create.'

Richard Madden, who plays Robb Stark, told the *Baltimore Sun* of his upcoming fate on screen, 'I'm so psyched about that scene. It's the most awesome cinematic scene. It's really awesome. I've not read that far in the books. I read season by season so I can keep surprising myself. I think that scene is something that's going to be done so brilliantly. That's something they're just going to nail. I've had so much time to become this character. I've got a great deal of respect for and ownership of this character.'

RHAEGAR

For a man considered to have been a fine king, Rhaegar was the central figure in the successful rebellion against his father Aerys II, which brought down the Targaryen dynasty on the Iron Throne.

He is an intelligent person, and, if slightly withdrawn, much loved by people who know him, including, surprisingly, Ned Stark. He is a skilled fighter, but he is also known for his music talents, singing mournful songs on his harp and often reducing women to tears.

Cersei was awed by Rhaegar, and her father tried to marry her off to him, but Aerys, the Mad King, refused to allow it.

He marries Elia Martell, and they have two children together. But at the Tourney at Harrenhal, he destroys everyone that would fight him, and, when he takes the winter rose crown for the Queen of Love and Beauty, he gives it to Lyanna Stark rather than his wife.

It is believed that Rhaegar kidnapped Lyanna, Ned's sister and betrothed to Robert Baratheon, for unknown reasons, and this triggered Robert's Rebellion.

Robert and Rhaegar have an epic fight at the Battle of the Trident, where a wounded Robert eventually strikes down the Targaryen with his hammer. Many believed he would have been a great king, and cannot believe that he sabotaged his potential with the kidnapping.

However, there is a strong theory that the two were actually in love, and that they had a baby, which turned out to be Jon Snow. Robert's hatred for Rhaegar would have put the boy in danger, so Ned agreed to pass him off as his bastard son.

SANSA STARK

The eldest daughter of Catelyn and Eddard Stark, Sansa's journey from impressionable girl to hardened and cynical woman is one of the series' high points. Delighted at the prospect of marrying the handsome Prince Joffrey, she heads to King's Landing with her father and younger sister Arya.

During their journey, however, she sees the other side of her future husband – witnessing his cruel and vicious streak, as he taunts the travelling party's butcher's boy and attempts to strike Arya down before he is attacked by her direwolf. Forced to give her account of the incident in front of her father and Joffrey's family, she pleads ignorance, claiming she didn't see anything.

Upon learning of her father's supposed betrayal of the throne and forced to publicly denounce him as a traitor, she begs for mercy, and is seemingly given this by Joffrey, now King. However, Ned's reluctant confession to ensure the safety of his daughters is ultimately rejected by the young King, who to the shock of Sansa orders him beheaded.

After her father's death, she is summoned to see Joffrey, who gleefully shows her the severed head of her father in order to keep her in line. She composes herself, refusing to let him see her in distress. It's this inner strength that we see constantly during series two, as she is desperate to keep any feelings of hate and revenge secret, hidden deep within so as not to arouse any suspicion from prying eyes and ears in King's Landing.

She is frequently punished and publicly assaulted and taunted by Joffrey, usually upon hearing news of another victory battle by her brother Robb, who is leading a North rebellion against the Kingdom. But the recently appointed Hand of the King, Tyrion Lannister, is fond of young Sansa and demands an end to the brutality she is dealt.

Following the Battle of the Blackwater, she is freed of her wedding commitment to Joffrey, who will now marry Margaery Tyrell.

> **SPOILER**
>
> However, Sansa is forced to marry Tyrion, as part of a plan by Tywin to ensure he keeps her prisoner at King's Landing. The pair marry and, although incredibly disgusted by their union, she thanks him for not bedding her on their wedding night. When King Joffrey is murdered, she is rescued by Littlefinger, who tells her that he murdered Joffrey. She flees with him, and poses as his daughter.

Sansa Stark is played by Sophie Turner. Born on 21 February 1996 in Northampton, she had never acted on screen until she starred as Sansa in the HBO fantasy TV series. However, Turner had known she wanted to be an actress for as long as she can remember – having joined local theatre group Playbox in Warwick when she was just three years old.

'I always used to make up shows with my friends,' she told *winteriscoming.net*, 'mainly with my close friend Ellie Johnson but she soon got tired of it. I would always be the most crazy, the most loud out of all my friends and I used to channel that energy into dressing up and putting on shows. It's been a huge part of my life and without acting I would be lost.'

She was 13 when she auditioned for the role of Sansa

after hearing about it from a drama teacher who had put her forward. Her drama teacher hadn't expected it to lead anywhere – she just wanted her young pupil to experience an audition and meet people through the process.

One of those auditions involved the scene where she is shown her father's decapitated head. Recalling the audition, she said, 'In order to prepare for a scene as shocking and upsetting as that scene, I had to really remove myself from myself (if that makes sense) and be Sansa, not Sophie Turner acting Sansa, I had to be her. By doing this, it meant that, instead of Sophie seeing all these fake heads, Sansa was seeing all these real heads and so it all became a reality to me. I would often cry when I read the script for the scene because it was such a heartbreaking and horrific scene that it would really get to me.'

Constantly impressing the producers and George R. R. Martin, Turner finally found herself being screen tested with Maisie Williams – who would play her young sister Arya. They immediately high-fived and delivered an audition that sealed both of their lives on the show.

She said, 'I definitely think that we improved one another's performances because Maisie was and still is so good at what she does that I couldn't help feeding off that "annoying little sister" energy that she brought through in her performance and I think she fed off my "annoying older sister" energy that I was giving off, so it just worked.

We had a lot of chemistry that I hadn't had when I had auditioned with other Aryas. As soon as I entered the room and saw Maisie I gave her a high-five, asked her her name and we just clicked. After every take we would high-five each other and we gave each other a massive hug at the end, we were immediately friends.'

And Turner was certain Maisie would get the part. 'After my final audition, and my first audition with Maisie, I felt absolutely sure that she was going to be Arya, there was no doubt in my mind. It wasn't a matter of "Will Maisie get the part?" but "When will it be announced that Maisie has got the part?" I learnt that Maisie had got the part about two weeks after I found out that I had got the part via *winteriscoming.net* and I learnt that the lovely, talented Isaac [Hempstead-Wright] had got the part about two months after I learnt that I had got the part.'

Naturally, she felt nervous on her first day. 'It was a big scene as well – the King's arrival. And there's Sean Bean. It was overwhelming, but it was amazing.'

During breaks on the set, she sits in the trailer and plays I-spy with her mother. 'We point to Blu-Tack on the roof. It gets hideous. My mum has been an influence on me in the way that she is a very independent woman who never has to fall back or rely on other people and she can always find her own way. In the performing arts as a business, it is a very tough business, in which you have to learn to be independent and responsible very quickly and my mum taught me that from a very young age.'

There is a lot more to come from Sansa, and Sophie's immediate future will be on *Game of Thrones*. However, she is also looking beyond the series, stating, 'I have to say that I am incredibly excited for my future, especially if it involves *Game of Thrones*. I won't mind the attention because I suppose it comes with being in a television show, especially if it is as big as *Game of Thrones*! In the future, I don't really know which roles I would like, I'd like any role and I would dedicate myself to that role, as I have with Sansa. I don't tend to be fussy about the roles that I would like to be cast as, I really wouldn't mind… I like variety.'

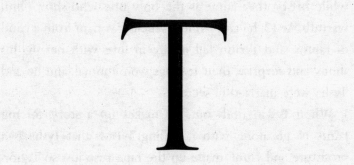

TYRION LANNISTER

Tyrion Lannister, or The Imp, as he's also known, is the youngest child of Tywin Lannister. He is also known as a half-man, and he possesses a caustic wit, sharp intelligence and a self-deprecating manner used to deflect abuse about his height.

He has also had to rely on a tough skin. Despite his family name, Tyrion is sometimes met with ridicule, and his father has always been unkind to him – blaming him for the death of his beloved wife, Joanna, who died giving birth to him.

His sister Cersei also shares the same contempt for him,

while his brother Jaime is the only one who shows him warmth. At 13, he and Jaime rescued a woman from a band of rapists, and Tyrion fell madly in love with her. To his shock and surprise, their feelings were mutual, and he and Tysha were married in secret.

When Tywin finds out, he makes up a story, forcing Jaime to go along with it, telling Tyrion that Tysha is a prostitute and Jaime made up the rape ruse just so Tyrion would finally get to sleep with someone. Tywin promptly has his entire guard rape her in front of Tyrion, making his son go last.

SPOILER

After he is made acting Hand of the King, following the events that led to Ned Stark's beheading, and showing good strategy skills, Tyrion shows considerable promise in taking out large portions of Stannis' army during his planned invasion of the King's Landing. But he is wounded by a member of the Kingsguard, and passes out. He later discovers that his father is seen as the saviour and he's now been demoted to Master of Coin.

Tyrion is forced to marry Sansa Stark by his father, but refuses to consummate the marriage.

Soon after, Tyrion is wrongly accused of the murder of King Joffrey, his nephew. He is condemned to death, but is rescued by his brother Jaime. During their escape, Jaime finally tells his brother the truth about Tysha – that she loved him and she wasn't a prostitute but a peasant girl. Tyrion is furious with Jaime and abandons him. He discovers one of the tunnels underneath King's Landing that leads to his father's room, where he promptly murders him.

He flees across the Narrow Sea, with Cersei offering a bounty for her brother.

During his journeys, he learns of a woman possessing dragons.

TYWIN LANNISTER

As the head of the Lannister family, you would expect nothing more than someone with a steely gaze and a heavy-set frame, who imposes himself over the headstrong family both physically and mentally. Cersei, Jaime and Tyrion aren't weak or lacking in bravado, yet it's clear that they fear their father, but also ultimately respect him, craving his attention like any other child.

Casting the role meant finding someone who could be authoritative and menacing. He is spoken of but not seen for a large part of the first series, and, while he has a bigger presence in the second series, his appearances are still fleeting. It needed an actor who could create such a dynamite presence that would linger long after he was gone.

Speculation on *winteriscoming.net* had almost all British actors up for the part.

If you're casting a British actor with a bald head, and one that has authority, then most speculation will concern Sir Patrick Stewart. The *X-Men* and *Star Trek: The Next Generation* star already has genre cred, and as a respected RADA actor he would have the requisite gravitas.

Popular British actor Bill Nighy – famed for romantic comedy *Love Actually*, animated smash *Rango* and the *Pirates of the Caribbean* – was also mooted, as was Australian actor Alan Dale. At one time best known for playing Jim Robinson on enduring Australian show *Neighbours*, Dale's move to America saw him land recurring roles in *The O.C.*, *24* and *Lost*.

Winteriscoming.net said about Nighy: 'Another easily recognisable actor, he doesn't however have quite the name recognition of Stewart. Still, Nighy has appeared in dozens of popular films over the past decade, including *Pirates of the Caribbean*, *Underworld* and soon-to-be popping up in the film series that seems to have employed all the best British actors over the past few years, *Harry Potter*. Nighy doesn't quite have the look I imagined for Tywin, but the actors they cast for Jaime and Cersei weren't a perfect fit either and that seemed to work out just fine. They'd have to see what he looks like bald first, but I think they could make it work.'

While the website said about Dale: 'The only non-Brit on this list, Dale was born in New Zealand and started his acting career there and in Australia. He starred on the Australian show *Neighbours* for eight years and after leaving there decided to move to the States. Since then he has appeared on quite a few popular US TV shows, including *The O.C.*, *Ugly Betty*, *Lost* and HBO's own *Entourage*. He looks most like how I imagined Tywin to look, just slap some mutton chops on him and he would be perfect. Despite not being British he most likely does belong to British Equity (an important element to getting cast it seems) as he starred in the West End production *Spamalot*. We'll see if that is enough to get him cast.'

Dale in particular possessed all that was needed for the part, but so did the actor that eventually landed the part.

Charles Dance is a veteran TV actor, best known for playing the villain in Hollywood blockbusters *Golden Child* and *Last Action Hero*. He was also mentioned on w*interiscoming.net*'s list, and there was little wonder. He was exactly what was needed for the role of Tywin Lannister.

'I avoid reading books that are that thick!' Dance commented to *westeros.org*. 'They frighten me, and they weigh a lot in the baggage as well. No, I stick to the script because that's what we're dealing with, and the scripts happened to be really, really good. If, while working on this, I thought the scripts were not very good, I'd go back to the source material and try to figure out why that was the case. But the writers on this have been very clever. The quality of the writing is as good as the quality of the production values, which, for a television show, are astonishing. I didn't realise how widely read the books are, I really didn't. I hadn't heard of them before. Someone told me, "Oh, it's a kind of grown up *Lord of the Rings*," which it is because there's more rumpy-pumpy! And it is quite violent. But I'm kind of continuously surprised because they are very widely spread, and they will be more so now because, like all literary adaptations, the one service an adaptation will do for a book is to make people who've not read the book think, "Oh, now I'll read the book." Which is good, it's good for everybody.'

Tywin is the Warden of the West. He has a daughter Cersei and two sons – Jaime, who he adores because he's everything that he ever wanted as a son, and Tyrion, who he would happily have smothered, blaming him for the death of his beloved wife and his appearance.

Dance added, 'Much the same as playing any character, really. I pretend – that's what an actor's job is. But a man of his age, like a man of my age, you become increasingly aware of your mortality, but in this society life isn't a very expensive commodity. People get their heads chopped frequently in this. Although it's mythical, one can draw a parallel with medieval Europe, and life *was* cheap. Life is more valuable to us now, in the 21st century, but anybody who has any knowledge of history knows that one of the ways we have evolved is to value life more and live in a way that prolongs our life. Then, I think there was an acceptance that life was fine as long as it goes on, but when it stops, it stops. Because of my age, I have an ability to think myself into the state of a man who's going to be reminded of his mortality frequently.'

When asked his opinion of the character, Dance said, 'Yes I do like him, but I don't think he's a bad guy at all. No. He's a man of principle; they might not be your principles or my principles, but he's quite principled. But no, I don't always play the "bad" guy. I've played quite a few not "bad" guys. But if something as well written as this comes along.'

Lannister's rise as a controlling, ruthless, driven and punishing leader of House Lannister stems from his father, a gentle but weak man who was mocked by his bannermen.

'I'm attracted to characters that make you ask questions, or make an audience ask questions – why is he doing that, what is he really about? – that's great as far as I'm concerned,' Dance said. 'There's an ambiguity about him, you're never quite sure which way he's going to go. There are scenes where I have a fair amount of dialogue, but most of the time he is a man of few words and he doesn't smile very much either. I think he's a great character, but I wouldn't describe him as a bad guy, not at all.'

When Tywin imprisoned a disloyal bannerman, the wife of the bannerman captured three Lannisters and threatened to harm them if her husband was not released – something that his father did, much to the shock of Tywin, who had told him to send the man back in three pieces.

The House was becoming a joke, and when Tywin took over the House he made sure he took care of the worst dissenters: destroying the line of House Tarbeck and House Reyne completely.

He married his cousin Joanna, who is said to have ruled his home with the same iron fist that he himself did at Casterly Rock and the Seven Kingdoms as Hand of the King to Aerys, who was impressed by the 20-year-old.

He did such a good job as the Hand for 20 years that people began spreading the word that the Hand was the real King. This would prompt anger from Aerys, aka the Mad King, who would begin to resent his right-hand man. After Tywin's proposal to have his daughter Cersei marry the King's heir Prince Rhaegar was rejected, and as his 15-year-old son, Jaime, had been taken away from him to the Kingsguard, he resigned as the Hand and headed back to Casterly Rock.

During Robert's Rebellion, Tywin ignored Aerys' order to help, refusing to take sides. However, after the rebellion scored a key victory at the Battle of the Trident, he rode to King's Landing with his forces, and promptly sacked the city – with Tywin's knights slaying Rhaegar's wife and her two young children, who Tywin wrapped up in Lannister cloaks and gave to Robert as an oath of loyalty.

He was repaid, with Cersei marrying King Robert, meaning Lannister had a legitimate claim to the throne.

He would constantly lend money to the Crown because of King Robert's financial mismanagement of the realm.

SPOILER

Tywin is eventually killed by his son Tyrion, after he finds his ex-whore, Shae, in his dad's bed. Tyrion strangles her with the golden chain that belongs to his father. He then takes a crossbow and shoots his father. Dance didn't know his character was going to be killed off, and by his 'son', until fans told him. He said, 'I do know [now], because devotees of the books approach me in the street and tell me all about it. So, I know now. It's quite something.'

USURPER

The War of the Usurper is commonly known as Robert's Rebellion.

Robert Baratheon, also known as the Usurper, is a vulgar, overweight, bitter and angry man when we first meet him in episode one.

He speaks warmly of Lord Eddard Stark, but the rest are there for nothing more than for him to insult and look down on. Unless you're a buxom wench, that is, in which case he will more than likely have his way with you, making sure his wife Cersei Lannister sees or hears about it through her brother Jaime, who he makes sure guards his door when he has female company.

It wasn't always that way. Cersei herself says near the end of the first series that Robert Baratheon used to be a mighty warrior and a muscled heartthrob who tore through the Seven Kingdoms to depose of the Mad King.

But being King was not what fed this mighty warrior, so he indulged himself in other ways – namely drinking copious amounts of alcohol and gorging at the many feasts that he would demand be named in his honour. He even grew a beard to hide his many chins.

Robert was born to Lady Cassana and Lord Steffon Baratheon, with a brother Stannis arriving a year after him and a second sibling, Renly, coming several years after that. His grandmother was a Targaryen.

When he was young, he saw his parents die in a shipwreck and he was forced to become the Lord of Storm's End; he made a fine hand at it, thanks to Stannis' help.

Robert goes to live with Jon Arryn, and during this time he becomes friends with Eddard Stark; he also meets and falls deeply in love with Eddard's sister Lyanna. After Lyanna is kidnapped by Rhaegar Targaryen, Eddard's brother Brandon and his father Richard head to King's Landing seeking justice. Richard is burned alive, while Brandon is hooked up to a device that strangles him the more he struggles as he watches his father die.

Jon Arryn is ordered to give up Robert and Eddard, but he refuses, instead starting the rebellion with both of them. Robert soon becomes the leader of the revolt – which became known as Robert's Rebellion.

He faces a rebellion of his own at Storm's End, with some of his bannermen refusing to join the rebellion and deciding to stay loyal to the throne. He finds out that the lords of the Houses Fell, Cafferen and Grandison are to join up at Summerhall, but Robert and his forces rush to quell the rebellion, winning three battles in one day, with Robert also killing Lord Fell in single combat.

The Battle of the Trident sees Robert face off against Rhaegar, who is convinced of Robert's guilt in the kidnapping of his beloved Lyanna. Their battle is an epic one, and Robert is wounded, but he is ultimately victorious, killing Rhaegar with his giant hammer. Lyanna dies during the conflict, forcing Robert to head to the Red Keep with vengeance in his heart.

When Tywin presents Robert with the bodies of his arch nemesis's wife and two children, he is pleased they are dead – much to the disgust of Eddard. Robert simply replies that he sees no babes, only dragon spawn.

The incident threatens to force a wedge between the two friends, and rears its head once again after Ned refuses to sanction the murder of Daenerys' child.

Stark leaves and heads to Storm's End to help a besieged

Stannis. Their shared grief at the death of Lyanna brings them back together.

With the shrewd help of Jon Arryn as his Hand, they pardon the rebellion's many enemies, and forge alliances with those that wanted to kill them. Some are more reluctant to forge alliances than others – with Dorne outraged that Robert condoned the murders of Rhaegar's wife and children.

Robert marries Cersei Lannister, but their marriage is doomed from the start, with Robert whispering 'Lyanna' on their wedding night.

Robert is an unhappy man, but, six years after being named King, he joins forces with Eddard to crush the Greyjoy rebellion.

He dies at the end of season one, not knowing that his children were in fact not his but his wife's brother's.

Robert is played with much gusto by Mark Addy.

'They sent me about three or four scenes to learn for the audition and I thought, "This is actually really good stuff,"' Addy told *Access Hollywood*. 'Then subsequently, I went and bought the book and thought, "This is a really good book." So it was great to have the opportunity of being part of something that is such a huge and beloved thing.

'It's a little bit of everything really. The fact that George has written such extraordinarily rich characters that are described in the finest detail in the books gives you a really, really strong framework on which to create your own version of that.'

The costumes also played a part. 'Physically, the kind of costumes that they made for us helped,' he explained. 'Once you get into that gear, it sort of gives you a feeling of who that person is, and then you've got directors who know the books, know the characters as well as we do, so they wouldn't let you get away with anything that was too far away from who these people are.'

He continued, 'You kind of figure out what makes a person, the way George has written such great history. Your entire backstory is right there for you. In the books, you find out what these guys are like as boys growing up into men and assuming positions of power, which they're probably not best suited for, and consequently being involved in a loveless marriage, which is really more of a political move than borne out of any kind of real feeling for the other person. It all combines to create somebody who is a very flawed character who has turned to the drink [and] the whores in order to kind of keep himself sane.'

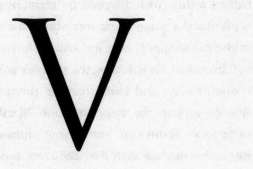

VAMPIRES

Zombie-like creatures and vicious monsters may bump in the night Beyond the North Wall, but, in 1982, Martin used a different supernatural foe for his book *Fevre Dream*.

Inspired by teaching at a girls' school that overlooked the Mississippi River, Martin crafted a book that is becoming more and more beloved as readers of his fantasy series track down the writer's earlier work. Unbelievably, this supernatural gem went out of print for two decades before it was reissued following the success of *A Song of Ice and Fire*.

The book is set in 1857 on the Mississippi River, where steamboat captain Abner Marsh meets a rich gentleman named Joshua York. Plagued by financial problems, Marsh is promised a magnificent steamboat that will be the pride of the Mississippi River, and will be financed by York.

Christened *Fevre Dream*, the steamer is a majestic beauty – one of silver and blue, charging through the river. The two co-captain the ship, but soon Marsh begins having suspicions about his mysterious financial benefactor, suspicions that are shared by the crew and passengers.

York and his friends rarely venture out of the ship during daylight, and when Marsh finds scrapbooks of mysterious deaths in York's cabin he confronts him. Eventually, York confesses that he is a vampire. However, he has developed a 'cure' for the disease and he plans to free his people from their bloodlust. His group hail him the Pale King, but he is usurped after an evil vampire group led by Damon Julian board the boat and overpower him.

Damon takes over the *Fevre Dream*, and an obsessive Marsh spends years trying to track his beloved boat. Now an old man, Marsh receives a letter from York asking him for his help in defeating Julian.

The novel was dubbed 'Bram Stoker meets Mark Twain', and was nominated for both the Locus and World Fantasy Awards in 1983. Celebrity fans of the book include acclaimed horror director Guillermo Del Toro.

Martin told *Empire*, '*Fevre Dream* is my only vampire novel. I do have some ideas for a sequel to that book, which

I've had for decades. It's a question of finding the time to write it, and whether I will. I don't know if I ever will. I had always wanted to write something about vampires, going all the way back to the beginning of my career. For some reason, when I thought about vampires, having read *Dracula* and all that, it always seemed to me that it had to be a period piece, it couldn't be modern day. But again I didn't want to do something that had been done before; I wanted it to be something original.'

Martin continued, 'It began to gel for me in the late '70s when I took a job teaching college in Dubuque, Iowa. Dubuque is an old river town on the Upper Mississippi, when the steamboats used to ply their trade, and I got interested in the history of the place and suddenly it seemed to gel for me. Vampires and steamboats: there was a certain dark romanticism to both, and as far as I knew, no one else had ever done vampires on steamboats, and *Fevre Dream* was the result.'

He added that to a certain extent vampires seemed to work with steamboats. 'It was sort of a dark romanticism for both of them, which seemed to go together. There were certain aspects that didn't go together; most notably that vampires can't cross running water, according to the tradition, which would blow the whole thing right out of the Mississippi. So I said, "Well, I can't go with that, I've got to get rid of that aspect."

'And then once I got rid of that, I said, "Well, let me rethink the vampires and make them more rational vampires, more science-fiction vampires, not living corpses that are cursed because, you know, they have no souls or whatever their traditional supernatural thing is." A more science-fiction approach, a more realistic approach. And once I did that, they fit perfectly with the whole vampire riverboat thing.'

It was arguably his most famous book before *A Song of Ice and Fire*, and had been optioned for a movie adaptation – with Martin even writing a screenplay. Instead, it was adapted for a different medium.

'The head of Avatar Comics called me up and wanted to do some [comics based on] my work,' Martin explained. 'They wanted *Ice and Fire*, but I haven't sold any comic rights to *Ice and Fire*. People keep approaching me, I may do it some day, but it's such a big project, I don't know how they would do it.

'But we got to talking about other stuff, and I said, you know, *Fevre Dream* would probably make a good comic series.'

VARYS

Every political counsel has one, a figure who plays people with ease and weaves lies and manipulation through the corridors of powers. In *Game of Thrones*, there are two characters with such devious powers – Littlefinger and Lord Varys, the latter also named The Spider.

His spy network consists of many eyes that roam King's Landing; he refers to them as his 'little birds'. No one in the palace knows where they stand with Varys such is his skill at pitting people against each other and providing information to all sides.

Ned Stark is understandably reluctant when he first meets the Eunuch, Varys, a tag he wears with unease. As befits a man who you can never really trust, we only have his word about where he came from and it could all be just another lie from a man to whom duplicity comes as easily as breathing.

Varys was born to a life of slavery in Lys, one of the nine Free Cities. Surrounded by crushing waves and stormy seas, it is home to alchemists who, among many potions, make the ultra-rare poison 'the Strangler', a liquid that will crop up in a later series.

According to Varys, he was sold to a group of travelling performance artists and spent his time visiting the other Free Cities and also King's Landing. He was later sold to a man who used him as part of a Blood Magic ritual, giving Varys a potion that made him unable to move or speak. However, his senses were very much alive and he felt every excruciating second of pain as his manhood was sliced off.

Tossed out in the Free City of Myr, Varys resorts to begging and other dubious means to survive, and quickly realises he is a skilful thief. After teaming up with a Sellsword named Illyrio Mopatis, they start a venture where Varys steals precious objects from thieves, and Illyrio retrieves them for their previous owners for a small fee. It makes them very rich, and their wealth continues to grow through his very first spy network. Realising that information is the key to power, he recruits his 'little birds' – orphans that can sneak around tight spaces and get into corners unseen where they can eavesdrop on the wealthy and powerful and steal information.

King Aerys hears of Varys' talents and recruits him. He becomes the spymaster in King's Landing, and fuels the Mad King's paranoia, pointing out traitors and those that manipulate others in the area.

He advises Aerys to close the gates to his former Hand Tywin Lannister, convinced that he cannot be trusted. But the Mad King refuses to listen to the Eunuch, choosing, instead, to seek advice from Grand Maester Pycelle, and opens the gates to Lannister's 12,000-strong army.

It proves to be a fateful mistake. Despite pledging allegiance to the Targaryen cause, Lannister's army pillages the city in the name of King Robert's Rebellion. Aerys has feared this rebellion for some time, and has secretly placed the highly flammable wildfire underneath the city. His plan is to destroy the city, killing millions of its citizens rather than have the rebellion win. However, Jaime Lannister stops it from happening, slaying the King inches away from the Iron Throne.

Varys keeps his post when King Robert reclaims the throne, but he and Illyrio Mopatis maintain their loyalty to House Targaryen.

They swap Rhaegar's baby son, Aegon, with a peasant baby, and secretly smuggle him across the narrow sea. It's seemingly Varys' desire to see Aegon reclaim his throne and restore the Targaryen line to the Iron Throne. But wicked whispers and an over-reliance on spies is one thing – eventually, Varys must get his hands dirty to move things forward, and that he does.

SPOILER

In the book *A Storm of Swords*, we see Varys testifying against Tyrion, who is falsely accused of murdering King Joffrey. Providing damning evidence through detailed notes of their conversations, his testimony plays an integral part in the decision to sentence him to death.

Jaime Lannister forces Tyrion to rescue his brother, and they do so, thanks to the secret tunnels beneath the Red Keep. They pass a ladder that leads up to the room of Tywin. Despite Varys' protestations, Tyrion heads up there to kill his father.

> Varys returns to the secret passages at a later date, and kills Kevan Lannister. Kevan is a bright man who is helping Tommen command the role as King with respect, and has canny leadership skills. Unfortunately, that could hinder his chance to get Aegon to reclaim the throne. He kills Kevan with a crossbow, telling him that it's not personal but that his leadership skills threaten to unravel years of hard work, and that his death will further antagonise tensions between House Tyrell and House Lannister.

On 15 July 2010, George R. R. Martin announced on his blog: 'And to confirm the story that Mo Ryan broke earlier today in her column, the role of Varys the Spider will be played by Conleth Hill.'

His casting at first raised eyebrows from fans – he was an unknown entity. Bean, Dinklage and several others were well known. And, as Varys was such an integral character to the series, they had expected a bigger name.

Of course, now they couldn't see anyone other than Hill playing the part. He remains reluctant to give interviews and is rarely seen promoting the show; he seems to enjoy doing his work and then going home – but perhaps that is just right for the character of Varys. The most mysterious man in *Game of Thrones* is played by the most mysterious actor in *Game of Thrones*.

While Hill stays in the shadows, he lets others spread the word about the show and does his work for them – his fellow actors... his little birds.

WAR OF THE ROSES

Martin had grown tired of fantasy novels that he felt were nothing more than Tolkien imitators writing 'Disneyland Middle Ages'. A keen history buff, he said, 'I wanted to capture these two threads to get some of the magic and the wonder and imagination of fantasy and combine it with some of the grittiness and realism and complexity of historical fiction.

'I saw Hadrian's Wall for the first time in 1981. It was on the occasion of the first time I'd ever been to the UK, and in fact I think the first time I'd ever left the United States. I was travelling with my friend Lisa Tuttle, who collaborated with me on the novel *Windhaven*. She had moved to the UK and married a British man, and she was showing me around. We were driving around the country and we reached Hadrian's Wall and it was sunset – it was at the end of the day, so all the tour buses were leaving. We saw people getting on their buses and going away because it was just about to get dark. We really had the wall to ourselves, which I think was great because it was the fall, and it was kind of a crisp, cold day. The wind was blowing, and I climbed up on the wall and it was really just awesome... So that was a profound experience that stayed with me. It was over a decade later when I first began *Ice and Fire*, and I still had that vision and that sense of, "I'd like to write a story about the people guarding the end of the world."'

Martin continued to explain the effect Hadrian's Wall had on his ideas, and the impact historical influence has on his writing. 'But, of course, in fantasy you always play with these things. Fantasy is bigger and more colourful, so a mere 10-foot-high wall wasn't going to do it for me. My wall is 700 feet tall and made of ice. And the things that come out of the north are a good deal more terrifying than Scotsmen or Picts, which is what the Romans had to worry about.'

Medievalism was something of a massive influence on Martin, especially the period between 1455 and 1487 in

England – dubbed The Wars of the Roses. They were a series of civil wars between the House of Lancaster and the House of York, with the name derived from the badges used by the two sides: one a white rose, the other red.

X-RATED

You know you're a part of pop culture when you've been parodied, and, in a famous *Saturday Night Live* sketch, the show poked fun at *Games of Thrones*' many scenes of nudity. The central joke was that there was a teenage consultant on the show to ensure there were just enough 'boobies'.

The show certainly has had its fair share of complaints about nudity. Nothing new for HBO, but one blogger claimed that the show's bosses had managed to create something new with male and female nude scenes. Dubbing it 'sexposition', Myles McNutt coined the term to describe the amount of plot details and backstory through the scenes.

Time Magazine critic James Poniewozik added, 'It's something more than gratuitous or ample sex and nudity in a show – it's using that sex to divert the audience or give the characters something to do in scenes that involve a big download of information or monologue. I wouldn't say *Game of Thrones* is the first. I think of all the *Sopranos* scenes in the Bada Bing, with strippers on the pole while two characters discuss plot points, or *Deadwood*, when Al Swearengen would deliver long monologues to a whore who was fellating him.'

British cinema historian Matthew Sweet noted, 'The nudity in *Game of Thrones* goes back to something even older – a classical context meant nudity was permissible and casual and everyday, and that comes from 19th-century painting.'

So what's new about the new wave of nudity? 'What may be different here is that you didn't have as much need for exposition in past TV shows,' Sweet continued. 'In the '70s, when [cinema] producers had to be very aware of giving their audience the things they couldn't get on TV, producers would say to the writer, "We need nudity and a murder before the titles." The rules of screenwriting laid that down quite forcefully. You'd think HBO could be free of those diktats, but they're not – they're giving you something that's not available on free-to-air TV. This is premium TV, but it gives you the same thrill that you got from '70s exploitation movies.'

Questions about the nudity are aimed at Benioff a lot, and he joked one time, 'We will address this issue with a 20-minute brothel scene involving a dozen whores, Mord the Jailer, a jackass, and a large honeycomb.'

Weiss added, 'There will always be those who want to see less sex, and those who want to see more sex, and those who want to see sex in big tubs of pudding. You just can't please everyone. This year, we're going to focus on the pudding people.

'There's not a checklist. You just have to do what feels right to you and not worry too much about it. [You don't] start counting how many breasts per episode or how many full-frontal male nudity shots. There are always going to be people who think there's too much. There will be some who want to see less. One of the benefits of HBO is that we can give a more well-rounded representation of life. And that sex is a part of it and darkness is a part of it, and so is the humour.'

According to Benioff and Weiss, the character of Ros – played by Esmé Bianco – was originally created as a plot device, allowing them to bolt the many scenes that happen in whorehouses and to prostitutes to one central character.

'There's definitely something to be said for the fact that

she's a common thread between all of these people, which I don't think any of them realise,' said Bianco. 'People are unguarded around her, which will prove to be interesting. There's a person beyond the plot device. She's a cocky girl, and there's no denying that. She knows how far she can push it, but she knows at what point society is not going to ever accept her. The problems that she faces are very representative of the problems that women face today, but you hope that not too many women are forced to beat their co-workers with a large stag-headed sceptre.'

Bianco is a famed burlesque dancer, but insists she doesn't want to be just known as 'that naked girl'. 'Objectivity is almost a choice you make. As a burlesque performer, I didn't choose to be objectified. I'm entertaining people, and people can choose to see me as an object because I'm naked, but I don't choose to see myself like that. I hold the power.'

Bianco added, 'When there's a naked woman on the screen, people start making judgements about it. I've been over here [in Los Angeles] since *Game of Thrones* came out, so I don't know how different the reaction has been in Europe, where people are a lot more tolerant of nudity on screen. People [here] see a pair of breasts, and they forget that there's a story going on.'

Not all actresses were eager to disrobe, with one actress turning down the part because of the nudity. Irish model/

actress Lisa Nolan was cast for the second season, but she said, 'The scene looked like it was going to basically be soft porn. I thought it wasn't a sex scene and they said they would give me skin patches for my breasts. But when I got there they wanted me to be fully topless and in the scene I had to strip off. So I pulled out at the last minute.'

Emilia Clarke herself said about taking on the part of Daenerys, 'When I first auditioned, they said there might be a bit of nudity (a smidgen). It was only on a family holiday prior to filming that I got the full final draft of the script through, and had a jaw-to-the-floor shock and petrifying moment. I'd read the books and I loved Daenerys, and I knew what I needed to do to get the integrity of the role across and what the audience needed to see to glean the empathy that was required to do Dany proud. I just as an actor threw myself into it in that sense. HBO were there to catch me, they are incredible! Really tasteful – you put your trust in them and it pays off. Also, Jason Momoa is an all-time legend and was just certainly so easy.'

Peter Dinklage has no problem with filming the sex scenes. 'Those scenes are fun,' he said. 'We get so much flak for it, but what's wrong? I just find it to be so sad, people get in such an uproar about breasts, but not chopping people's heads off.'

Author Martin himself said, 'I get letters about that fairly regularly. It's a uniquely American prudishness. You can write the most detailed, vivid description of an axe entering the skull, and nobody will say a word in protest. But if you write a similarly detailed description of a penis entering a vagina, you get letters from people saying they'll never read you again. What the hell? Penises entering vaginas bring a lot more joy into the world than axes entering skulls.'

YGRITTE

A flame-haired feisty woman, whose hair is described by her wildings family as having been 'kissed by fire', Ygritte is part of a scouting party that is ambushed by a team of Night's Watch members, which includes Jon Snow.

Lord Eddard's bastard child is told to kill her, but, as they leave him to do the job, she seizes on his reluctance and tries to escape.

SPOILER

Snow manages to capture her, but he is lost from his group in the vast wilderness. She is eventually found

---

by her wilding companions, and is happy when Jon says that he wants to turn his back on the Night's Watch to join the wildings. Unbeknown to them, Snow is undercover in a bid to infiltrate them.

They eventually begin sleeping together, which goes against his Night's Watch vow. However, when he is told to kill a lone knight, he refuses, and Ygritte ends up slitting the knight's throat. Jon attempts to flee, and his lover shoots him in the leg with an arrow.

He manages to get to Castle Black, where he successfully sees off the wildings. Ygritte is killed in the attack, dying in Jon's arms.

ZOMBIES

Well, not really zombies, but wights.

Wights are deceased bodies brought to life by the White Walkers. Unnervingly strong, they can survive the most brutal of attacks, and will still attack even if some of their limbs are missing. However, they are susceptible to fire.

As Kit Harington said, 'The way I think of it, the Others, or the White Walkers, are this ancient race of people, and they use the zombies, or the wights, to be their army. But they're not as bad-ass as the White Walkers are. I think that's what's so fascinating about this series, and especially the new season, because there's something stirring in this world, and the fantasy elements are going to play a much bigger part. We opened the first season with the White Walkers, but then they went away. And now we have the feeling that something is changing. We've got dragons, magicians, witches, zombies, loads of different elements, all coming in a subtle way; we're not smacking you in the face.'

EPISODES GUIDE

WINTER IS COMING

Season one, episode one
Written by David Benioff and D. B. Weiss
Directed by Tim Van Patten

HBO's Michael Lombardo had typically raved about it, critics foamed at the mouth proclaiming it the must-see TV event of the year, while fans of the series eagerly awaited the show they thought they would never see – and on 17 April 2011, two weeks after HBO had already teased fans with a 15-minute preview running on websites, it finally arrived.

'Winter is Coming' begins with a bang. The men of the Night's Watch ride out Beyond the Wall to capture tribes of wildings. They find the bodies of men, women and children dismembered in the cold woods. One of the rangers flees and is captured outside the castle wall of Winterfell and is immediately deemed a deserter. The punishment is swift and severe, a beheading by Lord Eddard 'Ned' Stark.

In the original script, it is stated that King Robert and the King before him had hired someone specifically to do the beheading. However, Ned sees it differently, telling his young son Bran, 'The man who passes the sentence should swing the sword.'

Stark later finds out that his mentor, and the Hand of the King, has died. King Robert is soon to pay Stark a visit, which can mean only one thing: the King will ask his old friend to become his new Hand. Stark is reluctant to take the position, but, when he finds out that his mentor was murdered and that the King is in danger, he says yes to the offer. One of his young sons, however, accidentally walks in on the King's wife and her twin brother having sex in an abandoned tower. He is caught by the brother, Jaime Lannister, and pushed to the ground.

TRIVIA

The wildings at the start were merely piled up on top of

each other in the pilot, but in the reshoot it was decided to go for a more horrific image.

The dead stag seen near the start was a real dead one, and was decomposing so badly that a crew member vomited.

The direwolves were introduced early on in the episode, and obviously feature heavily in later episodes, but Martin wasn't a fan of how they looked in the first series. While they used Northern Inuit dogs that were specifically bred to look like wolves, they did not carry the same intensity and, according to the author, 'actually caused problems because the dogs were too nice'. Instead of baring their teeth and growling, they would instead wag their tails and lick people's faces, dulling their impact to such an extent they were excised from certain scenes. Season two saw the introduction of real wolves, albeit in controlled conditions.

Other times they used CGI (computer-generated imagery) wolves, with Martin noting, 'We're getting something much closer to what I imagined in the books in terms of size and ferocity and the danger of the wolves.'

Alfie Allen's hair is dark in the series, but they used his natural blond roots in the pilot, and there are glimpses of this different hairstyle from the pilot retained for this episode. 'I had some bow-and-arrow experience from when I was a kid but other than that, nothing serious,' he told *GQ* magazine. 'Drawing it was tough, man. But it was cool. At one point I got four bullseyes in a row and was really proud of myself. I had to stop mid-scene.'

The courtyard is normally a gift shop in real life, while the Winterfell crypts are really a wine cellar.

Sophie Turner, who plays Sansa Stark, told *winteriscoming.net* about her first day of shooting, 'My first day on set involved a lot of squeals of excitement on my part. It was a scene which involved many extras so I was very nervous with so many people around but everybody (the cast, crew and extras) were all so welcoming, friendly and helpful that I settled down and felt really at ease, even in front of the camera. That is when I realised that acting is what I really wanted to do. The most surprising thing was how considerate and lovely everyone was. I felt part of a massive family the moment that I stepped on set.'

Kit Harington, Richard Madden and Alfie Allen all held their breath to showcase their abs during the topless hair-cutting scene. Allen also didn't eat for two days before the scene was originally due to be shot – so imagine his frustration when the scene had to be moved back!

Of working with Kit, Allen said, 'Everyone just hung out with each other. One thing I would say is that I think, in any environment that you work in, there's always going to be one or two people who you don't like. But there just wasn't that on *Game of Thrones*. I know it sounds cheesy and clichéd but it was like a big family. Some of the show is funny but it's not funny in a light way, it's funny in a "I don't know if I should be laughing at this but I'm going to anyway". So to have a nice feeling on set and everyone just to be good with each other, it makes those dark moments easier because then it's not just dark the whole time. Contrast of emotions is definitely something interesting that you like to do as an actor.'

Benioff and Weiss reluctantly added dialogue between Arya and Sansa, reinforcing the fact that Jaime and Cersei were siblings, after early screenings saw people being confused about their relationship.

When Mark Addy, playing King Robert Baratheon, met the Stark children, his remarks to them were made up by him on the spot. Addy told *thevine.com* about that scene, 'I dismount and I walk up to Ned. There's a little exchange that ends up with me laughing. Every time I laughed the horse would do a bit of a whinny – every single time – so you had a courtyard full of people on their knees rolling about.'

Tyrion's introduction was a new scene added from the pilot, because he didn't originally appear until later on when the feast was taking place.

The Dothraki wedding scene was disrupted after the set was partially washed away by a gale from the sea.

Iain Glen, who plays Ser Jorah Mormont, is dubbed 'Jorah the Explorer' by the crew because of all the exposition he has to speak.

The dragon eggs that Daenerys receives ended up as a wedding present to Martin and his wife from Benioff and Weiss.

When Bran is pushed off the top of the castle, it's actually a stuntwoman who plummets to the ground.

POST-ANALYSIS

The reviews were almost universally positive, with *IGN* stating, 'As with any book adaptation, fans will worry and wonder as to what will be left out and what will be kept in, but the premiere episode not only effortlessly takes us along, faithfully, through the book, but it also manages to capture the majestically morbid spirit of Martin's pages and turn them into thrilling television.'

Time Magazine said the pilot was 'a very different one from many first episodes, even on HBO, in that it didn't so much tell a single story or establish symmetries among the subplots. Rather, it just set a very large table: a big welcome-to-Westeros that said boldly that no one here is safe.'

While *Den of Geek* website raved, 'On the basis of this first hour, the network has another hit on its hands that will not only please fans of Martin's work, but draw in new viewers, thanks to its realistic world, complex characters and good old-fashioned sex and violence. Winter may be coming, but *Game of Thrones* is here to stay.'

The initial ratings on its American debut were solid if not spectacular. It earned 2.2 million viewers, but impressively scored almost half than on its first repeat. The third screening drew nearly another million. Compared to HBO's *Boardwalk Empire*'s 4.8 million debut, it might have been seen as something of a disappointment. However, HBO dismissed the comparisons as the two were different breeds in both genre and star quality, with the prohibition drama starring Hollywood names and backed by the giant of mobster cinema Martin Scorsese. In fact, they warmed to the figures as the closest comparison they had was vampire noir *True Blood*, which only launched with 1.4 million viewers and went on to be a rousing success.

Coupled with successful UK debut ratings, a second season was commissioned shortly after its debut.

HBO's Michael Lombardo said in a statement, 'If you look at our history, it's very rare for us not to go to a second season, particularly on a drama like this. We're telling our subscribers, stick with this. In a few instances where we haven't allowed a show to go to a second season, our consumers tell us, please do that sparingly. We're going to do a show, you should get hooked on it. We believe in it, we're excited by it. We see a large part of our audience is. We lean into it, and we want the audience to lean into it as well.'

THE KINGSROAD

Season one, episode two
Written by David Benioff and D. B. Weiss
Directed by Tim Van Patten

Introducing a mass world that is coherent and throwing in a number of characters as quickly and seamlessly as possible is a problem many first episodes have to tackle. Unfortunately, given author Martin's love for new plot lines and characters at every turn, Weiss and Benioff face this problem with nearly every episode.

However, 'The Kingsroad', which debuted on 25 April

2011, saw them face an even more difficult challenge. After introducing the Starks in Winterfell, and hinting at complexities in the family – Ned's bastard son, Jon Snow, clearly not a favourite with Catelyn, the mother of Ned's other children, and typical teenage girl Sansa at odds with the more tomboyish Arya – the family are then split up.

Eddard Stark and his daughters depart for King's Landing, and head out on the Kingsroad. However, it turns nasty after Prince Joffrey – who is set to be betrothed to Sansa on the notion from King Robert that they should join their houses together – and Sansa take a walk on the riverbank. They find Arya toy fighting with the son of the party's butcher, and Joffrey takes offence that his betrothed sister is being seemingly manhandled. He begins to cut the terrified boy's face, but Arya defends him by hitting Joffrey with a stick. When Joffrey begins to attack her, her direwolf comes to the rescue and bites his hand.

After Ned is summoned to the see the king, the children each give conflicting events of the incident. However, despite Arya's direwolf escaping, it is judged that Ned's pet should be killed – to the horror of both Arya and Sansa, and to the delight of Cersei. Ned does the deed himself, and discovers that the butcher's son has been murdered. Meanwhile, Jon Snow has decided to join the Night's Watch, and heads to the Wall alongside a curious Tyrion Lannister, who has tagged along, desperate to see the huge structure.

Also in this episode, the Dothraki clan depart Pentos and head east, with Viserys Targaryen impatient at how long he'll have to wait until Khal Drogo launches his attack on the Seven Kingdoms. Daenerys is struggling with life with her new husband, and seeks advice on how to please him.

In Winterfell, while Bran lies unconscious after being pushed by Jaime Lannister, Catelyn stops an attack on her son's life, where a dagger is used to try and kill him. She then discovers a strand of blonde hair, similar to that of Cersei, at the tower where Bran fell.

TRIVIA

Talking about the differences in dress sense between the Starks and Lannisters, costume designer Michele Clapton told *onscreenfashion.com*, 'When looking at different groups, for example the Lannisters in the south and the Starks of the north, both are important families so we would look at what is available to them and what is important to their character. The Lannisters are very wealthy, competitive, they live in the capital and power is important. It's warm on the coast, which means there is trade and they don't have to worry about keeping warm. They have a large staff with silks and jewels readily available to them. As Cersei influences the court, and we notice her hatred for her husband, through season two we start to see her style begin to shift as her role changes.'

The Starks, however, live very differently, she continued. 'They have less available to them and are in different circumstances as they live in cold, damp weather. Available to them is wool, leather, fur and some dyes. They have to think about warmth and wear the high padded embroidered collars as status rather than jewellery. The village people wear a simpler form of this look. They are not ostentatious and are a loving family who are not trying to prove anything. Only Sansa disagrees with this and we see this as she is influenced in her clothing, mainly by Cersei, and as the plot develops, she moves away from this.'

The scene where Cersei confronts Catelyn with a moving monologue about the death of her first son was Lena Headey's audition piece. During the commentary on the episode she also states that she believes that a young Cersei was unlike Sansa.

Mark Addy and Sean Bean have a couple of great scenes in this episode. 'We were in drama school at the same time, but we were in different years,' Addy said. They had previously worked on the acclaimed *Red Riding* TV trilogy. 'We get on very well,' added Addy. According to Lena Headey, Sean Bean would constantly steal her sandwiches when they had lunch on set. Despite their on-screen distance, Addy was also close to Headey.

Jaime and Cersei's sexual sibling relationship saw the term 'Twincest' coined by fans of the series – something that tickled both the actors.

During rehearsals of the scene where Joffrey attacks Arya, actor Jack Gleeson refused to call Arya's character a 'cunt' – preferring instead to only use the vulgar term while shooting because he didn't want to upset the young actress.

The wolves woke the actors up constantly with their howling. And in the scene where Ned Stark has to kill the animal, Sean Bean, who played the character, grew frustrated that a scene, which should have taken a minute to shoot, took hours to complete because the wolf kept moving.

Mark Addy was delighted with the first two shows and how it had already attracted a huge fanbase, noting, 'I think what HBO have done is ground this in reality. It is fantasy, it's fantasy writing, but they've seen that in order to make it work, and to make it watchable by anybody, it needs to have a reality to it. It can't be "and then he turned himself invisible". There are elements of the supernatural here and maybe the odd bit of magic – but that's kind of on the periphery. The main thrust of the thing feels so grounded in a reality.'

Dark haired Emilia Clarke spends almost two hours getting her hair transformed – with her hair being braided, a bald cap put on and then her wig styled.

Jack Gleeson told *GQ* about his audition for Joffrey, 'I only had one audition, and the producers and writers were laughing at my performance because I was being so snotty and arrogant. They found it comical. I thought that was good. A big influence was Joaquin Phoenix in *Gladiator*. Sometimes when I'm sitting on my throne, I think of Phoenix sitting on his, with that smirk on his face. And I think my portrayal of Joffrey is very clichéd. It's something that's so easy to slip into because I've seen so many villainous characters on TV and onstage and in films. Joffrey is definitely informed by those performances.'

Sophie Turner admits she feels sorry for Gleeson, whose chilling portrayal belies his real life persona. 'I kind of wish he would do more television interviews so that people can see what he's really like,' she told *Vulture*, 'because there is so much hate for Joffrey, I feel protective of Jack now. If I were him, I'd be petrified that people would come up and slap me on the street! I should be his bodyguard.'

She added, 'He really is lovely. After our takes when he's mean to me, he'll come over and have a nice chat with me. It's kind of surreal. I had one particularly horrible moment with Joffrey, and then he came over afterwards and he said, "How are you?"'

POST-ANALYSIS

Reviews weren't as ecstatic as the debut episode, but still earned roughly the same ratings as the week before. Shifting some of the characters out of their comfort zones meant it didn't have the same dynamic thrust as other episodes, but many critics described it as solid.

New York Daily News stated, 'It's probably worth mentioning that sometimes *Game of Thrones* moves as slowly as a large army on foot and horseback inching its way across a bleak, endless, overcast Northern plain.

'Oh wait, that's exactly what it is, and what they're doing. All that said, fans of the acclaimed *Game of Thrones* books, or even fans of fantasy realms in general, will find much to admire and enjoy here. It's the sort of show, like *Lost*, in which fans can immerse themselves as deeply as they wish and always find clues that will take them deeper.'

LORD SNOW

Season one, episode three
Written by David Benioff and D. B. Weiss
Directed by Brian Kirk

Two hours into season one and finally we see King's Landing, with Eddard (Ned) and his daughters arriving after their long journey. We also have the first glimpse of Grand Maester Pycelle, Lord Petyr 'Littlefinger' Baelish, King Robert's brother Lord Renly Baratheon, and head of the king's intelligence network, Varys. It's clear that Ned is a leader of men, steeped in nobility and honour. However, his role as Hand of the King is alien to him. Cunning and manipulation of egos are required here, not courage.

Catelyn also arrives at King's Landing and is taken to one of the brothels that Littlefinger owns. With the help of Varys it's discovered that the elaborate dagger used to try and kill Bran once belonged to Tyrion.

There is also a more in-depth look at the Wall, having briefly witnessed its wonder at the end of 'The Kingsroad' episode. We are introduced to Castle Black, which houses the members of the Night's Watch – those that guard the Wall. Ser Alliser Thorne reluctantly praises Jon Snow's combat skills, but his arrogant swagger and false sense of superiority rankles the other recruits. However, by the end of the episode he has channelled that arrogance into teaching them how to fight properly.

Across the Narrow Sea, Viserys begins to see that his plan has flaws and is furious at seeing Daenerys' growing command and power over the Dothraki warriors. She later finds out that she is pregnant.

The episode ends with Arya receiving her first sword-fighting lesson from the flamboyant 'dance instructor' Syrio Forel – a light-hearted scene with a watching Ned bemused and proud of his feisty daughter, tempered by the dread that she could be needing to learn these skills not as hobby, but for survival sooner than everyone may think.

TRIVIA

This was the first episode of the series that wasn't directed by Tim Van Patten. Brian Kirk would become a series regular, and his TV credits include *The Riches*, *Brotherhood* and period drama *The Tudors*. The Irish filmmaker also directed the movie *My Boy Jack* (2007), which starred Daniel Radcliffe.

The opening of the episode sees Ned and his daughters arrive at King's Landing in glorious weather – but it had been raining heavily the night before and the chairs they are sitting on are soaking wet.

Mark Addy said about King's Landing to *thevine.com*, 'The scale of those sets! That's the beauty of being able to use the Paint Hall in Belfast where they used to paint and assemble huge ships. You could build an entire town in that space and shoot there.'

The episode is dedicated to the memory of Margaret John, who played Old Nan in season one and died in February 2011 before it aired. Creators Weiss and Benioff issued a statement: 'We were deeply saddened to hear about Margaret's passing. She was a warm and wonderful person, and she was completely fantastic in her scenes with Isaac. We wish she could see them... but many people will, and they will love her. We will miss her terribly.'

The iPhone game *Fruit Ninja* was used by many of the cast and crew, quickly becoming a craze on set. Harry Lloyd, who plays Viserys, was blamed for introducing the catchy game on set, with many competing with each other to attain the highest score.

During commentary on of the episodes, the young female Stark members Maisie Williams and Sophie Turner's nerves during read-through were soothed by actor Joseph Mawle. He told them that if acting were easy everyone would be doing it; so not to be worried if it gets so hard sometimes, adding that they wouldn't have got the job if they weren't good.

The cast constantly meet up and discuss in length their theories on who will eventually sit on the Iron Throne. 'We do!' Kit Harington confirmed to *thevulture.com*. 'We have fights in the bar about it. I don't mean we're beating each other up – it's pretty amicable – but we do get pretty excited about the whole thing. Everybody has a character they think should be on the throne, and if you're playing one of those characters, you secretly think it should be you. You have to have a fierce loyalty to your character.'

Another theory that everyone's constantly discussing is who is Jon Snow's mother, with many casting doubt over Ned being his actual father. Kit Harington, who plays the role, told *Vulture*, 'You just don't know. George knows and Dave and Dan may have an idea, but they don't tell me. I'm just as much in the dark as anyone. All I'll say is that it's interesting that a man with a moral compass like Ned Stark's would have had affairs and dalliances that resulted in babies outside of his marriage. That's my only question about it. As far as playing the part goes, Jon doesn't know, so I don't need to know. But that's what's so great about the books: So many people have so many theories! I mean, there are even theories about how Jaqen H'ghar in the second book is actually Arya's fencing teacher, Syrio Forel, in the first book.'

The character of Arya's instructor Syrio Forel is bald in the books, but producers decided not to shave actor Miltos Yerolemou's hair as his bouncy afro looked good on screen.

Maisie Williams learnt how to sword fight with her left hand to be like the character portrayed in the books. 'My mum and stepdad had read the first book by this time and filled me in on Arya's character, including the fact that she is left handed,' she told *winteriscoming.net*, 'It's not that they wouldn't let me read the books, I just don't have time to read much and when I do, it has to be school stuff mainly. They would read me parts that showed Arya's character. I started practising with my left hand before we started filming because I wanted to get it right but was not able to use my left hand all of the time because of camera angles, so Arya is now a little ambidextrous!'

POST-ANALYSIS

Despite the new surroundings and a host of new characters that would be integral to the series, the episode moved at a brisk pace, and critics seemed to be back on board following the somewhat lukewarm response to 'The Kingsroad' episode.

IGN noted, '[It] was dense and filled with tons of exposition and back-story, which may or may not have interested those new to this story, but I found myself hanging on every precious word.'

The ratings seemed to back that up as well, boasting a 10 per cent increase from last week – the highest yet of the series. It was given further credence as it aired in the US when news broke that Osama Bin Laden had been killed, and the whole nation was gripped by the live news reports.

CRIPPLES, BASTARDS AND BROKEN THINGS
Season one, episode four
Written by Bryan Cogman
Directed by Brian Kirk

'Cripples, Bastards and Broken Things' is a line uttered by Tyrion when asked by Rob Stark why he has gone to the bother of designing a contraption for the stricken Bran, which will enable him to walk again. 'I have a thing for cripples, bastards and broken things,' he smirks. It's an a apt title, as the episode, debuting on 8 May 2011 and scripted by Bryan Cogman, has scenes dominated by the series' 'broken characters' – in the more literal sense there are the scenes with Bran, but then you have the outsiders – Jon Snow the bastard son of Ned; Theon Greyjoy's back-story of being shipped out to Ned by his father after he was defeated in battle; the Night's Watch's Castle Black full of outcasts and desperate men seeking to reclaim a place in the world.

There is also more focus on the Targaryen dynasty, with a bravura scene featuring Varys and a prostitute. The insolence is still there, but the actor also shows the character's pain at having the life that was mapped out for him since he was born suddenly taken away. He believes that he should be king – it's his right and he wants it with every fibre of his being, no matter who he has to step on to get his way.

The scene is also one of the early examples of 'sexposition' – a term that is used for the scenes featuring a lot of dialogue being used to explain the back-story of the characters, but set against a backdrop of sex and nudity.

Another aspect of the story is the murder–mystery subplot, which sees Ned investigating Jon Arryn's death. Embarking upon his investigation, Ned begins to follow some of Jon's final footsteps, with the help of Littlefinger, and he soon finds himself meeting a young blacksmith's apprentice Gendry, played by *Skins'* actor Joe Dempsie.

TRIVIA

Bryan Cogman was originally Weiss and Benioff's writing assistant during the pilot episode, but he was eventually promoted to script editor and had the responsibility of looking after the story lore for the season, to make sure the series was doing justice to the book's mythology. Then, out of nowhere, he was asked to come up with a script for episode four. Thinking it was just a test, and that if he passed he might be in line to write an episode in the third or fourth series, he was stunned to find the day after handing in the manuscript that they would be using it.

Alfie Allen, who plays Theon Greyjoy told *westeros.org*, 'You have people around you, like Bryan Cogman, who help fill you in on the histories and the families and what has gone on there. I try not to make it as if I use the books just as the only source material; you have to make it your own things. Obviously getting into costume and so on helps get into character. But once you're there on set, it's cliché, but it just happens – you just do it. I don't have any particular rituals. One thing as an actor that you have to do – for me anyways – is to use the experiences you've had in your life and associate them with what you're doing on the screen. It can be quite unnatural, like, I've done film where I'm being tortured, and of course I've never been tortured in my life. But I was watching the torture scene in *Reservoir Dogs* and the actor in that did such a fantastic job with the desperation in his eyes, falling apart and still trying to hold it together. So I used that, I thought about it and used that quite a bit to help my performance. So I do draw on other performances, too. Because there's things that are utterly unnatural and you'd never have happen to you in life, unless you've had a very strange life.'

Kit Harington and Bradley John-West, who plays Sam,

were stranded after getting stuck in the Castle Black lift for over an hour after it suffered a mechanical failure −a nurse was called on set in case anything happened.

In the books Sansa learns how the Hound's face became burnt via the Hound himself. However, because of timing, it's Littlefinger that tells her in the series − a change that infuriated some fans, as they felt it was integral to Sansa's and The Hound's latter relationship.

The Hand's Tourney is not as grand as the one depicted in Martin's book or in Cogman's original script, which detailed the event with such lavish scenes that hundreds of extras would have been required for huge singing set pieces and countless lords paying their respect to the Queen. However, for budgetary reasons these scenes were excised.

When Ser Hugh of the Vale is killed, Sansa and Arya's reaction is real. The actresses weren't present at the rehearsal, and so they had no idea his death was to be so bloody.

Joe Dempsie originally auditioned for Jon Snow, and a year-and-a-half later he was eventually cast as Gendry − King Robert's bastard son. 'I didn't get very far and then when the series was commissioned,' he told *Digital Spy*. 'I auditioned for another two roles, before eventually being cast as Gendry. It was a really nice process, actually, even though you're auditioning for these different parts. You're not thinking, "God, what am I doing wrong? How come I'm not getting these roles? I really want to be involved in this." It just seemed like the creators, David Benioff and Dan Weiss, had identified people that they wanted to work with, and then it was just a case of which piece of the jigsaw you fitted.

'It all worked out really well in the end because a couple of the parts I'd auditioned for before aren't anywhere near as interesting as Gendry becomes, in the end. So I was really lucky to get spotted. Also, at the time of casting, I didn't possess the physical attributes they were looking for. I was supposed to be tall, muscular with thick black hair, and I was none of those things! So it was very nice that they saw past that and took a chance anyway.'

The King-Beyond-the-Wall, Mance Rayder, is first mentioned in this episode.

The huge book of lineages Ned reads was prepared by Cogman, who also wrote huge detailed pieces of other family lines that were never shot. He compiled the book through intense research of the books and internet fan sites.

The end scene, when Catelyn arrests Tyrion, was Michelle Fairley's audition piece.

POST-ANALYSIS

The ratings were higher than the previous week, posting 2.5 million viewers. The episode was also a hit with critics. Despite its heavy use of exposition, 'Cripples, Bastard and Broken Things' was roundly praised for just that – critics lauding how the large scenes of character's back-stories were delivered with invention and skill, making the mythology of the show the central focus in this episode.

THE WOLF AND THE LION

Season one, episode five
Written by David Benioff and D. B. Weiss
Directed by Brian Kirk

First aired on 15 May 2011, 'The Wolf and the Lion' is the episode where we are left in no doubt that Ned Stark's place in King's Landing is an unwelcome one. He is being watched and manipulated, a pawn in a deadly game he does not understand.

Sean Bean, the actor playing Ned, inhabits a canny sense of world weariness in this episode, playing him like a man that knows he is in a place he can't understand yet refusing to back down from what he believes is right. The King's Landing is no place for a man of honour – such men have the same life expectancy as a petty thief. To thrive you must have more than base instinct, and possess the skills of duplicity and betrayal.

He is faced with such duplicitous men in 'The Wolf and the Lion' – both Littlefinger and Varys are plotting something in the background that involves Stark. His daughter Arya stumbles into the dungeon and hears of a secret meeting between Varys and a man named Illyrio, and they talk about events that have been set in motion and that war is inevitable.

Ned is faced with a serious problem – Tyrion's capture by Catelyn Stark is sure to land him in a difficult situation. It doesn't help that his relationship with Robert is strained after Ned refuses to endorse his plan to assassinate Daenerys when it is discovered she has a baby inside her. Fearing her pregnancy will rally the Dothraki tribe to invade Westeros, Robert Baratheon wants her assassinated.

We first see Tyrion in this episode in the hills of the Vale, surrounded by Catelyn's 'army'. The diminutive Lannister realises that Catelyn's loud declaration at the Crossroads Inn that she will be riding for Winterfell was a decoy. He has little time to admire her cunning, realising that he is being taken to Lady Arryn – the sister of Catelyn and husband of Jon Arryn, the last Hand to the King.

They head into Eyrie's High Hall, where Lysa Arryn and her nine-year-old son, during breaks from sucking his mother's breast, hold court before ordering him to the sky cells – a dungeon where one of the walls is missing, and he faces a huge drop to his death.

The highlight of the episode, and indeed one of the strongest scenes of the entire series, features Cersei and Robert sharing an intimate chat. It moves from tactics to shared disappointments about the relationship, before Cersei shows a rare moment of letting her guard drop, and tells Robert that she has feelings for him – feelings that Robert can't say he shares nor, tellingly, even tries to fake to avoid hurting her feelings.

The episode ends with Ned Stark being accosted by Jaime Lannister's men outside Littlefinger's brothel and being stabbed by a Lannister guardsman.

TRIVIA

The title refers to House Stark's sigil (a grey direwolf) and the Lannister's lion sigil.

When Gregor Clegane decapitates his horse, it was done via a blend of puppet work and CGI effects.

The scene featuring Loras and Renly as lovers was never so forcefully shown in the novels, with Martin only hinting at it in the book.

Loras Tyrell is played by Finn Jones, who was also considered for the role of Jon Snow.

Robert's brother Stannis Baratheon, who appears in season two, is first mentioned in this episode.

One of the most intriguing scenes of the season paired Addy and Headey, as Robert and Cersei, as the two talked about what went wrong in their marriage and what could have been. 'Lena and I got on like a house on fire,' Addy told *Access*. 'We absolutely adore each other, so it was terrific to have a scene where I wasn't snarling, "Be quiet woman!" at her, and to get – from our point of view as actors – to get to explore a little bit more of what these characters are on a maybe slightly more personal level than the image they presented as the Monarchy was intriguing. That was a scene that David [Benioff] and Dan Weiss created. It was fantastic to have something like that to play and to really plunge the depths of who these people are.'

The episode is dedicated to animal trainer Caroline Lois Benoist, who died from swine flu.

POST-ANALYSIS

The episode kept with the series' upward trend, posting more than 2.5 million viewers in America, and was met positively by critics.

Time Magazine wrote, "'The Wolf and the Lion' is the strongest episode of the season yet. *Thrones* has put its pieces in place and is ready to start putting them into motion. It began to let its swords do the talking (with unfortunate consequences for at least one poor horse). And while there were some very significant scenes of talk, the dialogue went beyond Westeros History 101 to take the story in some *very* interesting directions. The most compelling scene to me, though it contained no bombshell revelations, was the fantastic heart-to-heart between Robert and Cersei, in which they share a laugh at the idea of their marriage – their bitter, convenient marriage – being the one thing that's keeping Westeros from falling back into civil war: "How long can hate hold a thing together?"'

A GOLDEN CROWN

Season one, episode six
Written by Jane Espenson, David Benioff and D. B. Weiss
Directed by Daniel Minahan

Eddard is visited by Queen Cersei and Robert, and Robert strikes at Cersei for not doing what he wants her to do.

Bran is nearly killed after he is threatened by wildings, but Theon and Robb arrive to save the day, and they keep a woman named Osha, one of the wildings, as their prisoner.

Daenerys attends a ritual, eating a stallion's heart, struggling at first with the raw meat but eventually swallowing it all, and it's declared that she will have a son – dubbed Rhaego in honour of her slain brother Rhaegar. He will be a great conqueror, it is announced.

Viserys is frustrated by the lack of progress with his plan and, after seeing how much the crowd adore Daenerys, he decides to leave, and attempts to steal his sister's dragon eggs. He is stopped by Jorah Mormont.

Tyrion is summoned by Lysa Arryn to confess his sins, but he still insists he had nothing to do with the murder of her husband. He demands to be trialled by battle and asks for his brother Jaime to be his warrior – a request denied. Instead, a man named Bronn, who had tagged along with Catelyn during her capture of Tyrion, volunteers, and duly kills the man he is up against – freeing a grateful Tyrion.

With Robert away on hunting duties, Ned Stark, as part of his King's Hand honours, takes on the temporary role of King, and his first task is to address the matters of Gregor Clegane, who is ravaging the Riverlands. He orders the arrest of the knight.

Eddard finally discovers the secret that killed Jon Arryn: the House Baratheon line shows that all the children have black hair, all that is apart from Cersei and Robert's children. They are blond, and their father is Jaime.

Viserys turns up at a feast for his sister, drunk and angry. He causes a scene, drawing out his sword, an offence that is punishable by death in the sacred city. He demands his golden crown, and Khal Drogo agrees. It is forbidden to kill while drawing blood, so, instead, Drogo melts his golden coins and crowns Viserys with the melting material, watching him burn alive.

TRIVIA

Jane Espenson was a writer for *Buffy the Vampire Slayer*.

The scene where Robert takes no for an answer and makes Ned become the Hand was Mark Addy's final scene. Sean Bean was actually suffering from flu in that scene, so his bedridden state was accurate.

Emilia Clarke was told that the horse's heart was made from a substance similar to Gummi Bears, one of her favourite snacks. However, it tasted disgusting to Clarke, and the retching scene didn't require any acting. 'It was kind of like congealed jam!' Clarke said to *heyyouguys.co.uk*. 'Sort of solidified jam but tasted of bleach with raw pasta running through it! I think it was very helpful of HBO to give me something truly disgusting so there was not much acting required. I think I ate roughly 28 hearts in total throughout the day's filming. Then the map that I was kneeling on had a lot of [remnants], and then there was the spit bucket that I was vomiting in quite a lot [laughs]!'

It's also Peter Dinklage's wife's favourite scene of the movie.

Ser Gregor Clegane's rampage through Riverlands was going to be screened, but was eventually cut because of budgeting and timing issues.

Some of the show's stars, including Peter Dinklage and Emilia Clarke, only read the books after they finish each season.

POST-ANALYSIS

Despite glowing reviews of this episode, it was the first time in the series that there were decreased ratings. Critics praised the episode, while also blasting Bean's character's naivety. *The Atlantic* wrote, 'Ned's principles are, as always, admirable, and he's clearly interested in justice. But the sad truth is that the lack of guile that makes him honourable also makes him a pretty poor king.'

YOU WIN OR YOU DIE

Season one, episode seven
Written by David Benioff and D. B. Weiss
Directed by Daniel Minahan

Poor old Ned Stark – he has to carry the burden of knowing not only that Joffrey isn't his best friend's son, but also that Joffrey's father is the brother of Joffrey's mother. Ned is also distraught after learning that Robert is mortally wounded by a boar.

Knowledge is power, boasts Littlefinger, plainly amused that he is counselling Stark. That's not Ned's way, and he decides to remove Joffrey and his mother from the throne, but not before telling Cersei that he knows everything.

It gives her enough time to come up with her own plan – namely ripping up Robert's decree that Ned is Protector of the Realm until Joffrey is an adult. Ned, thinking he has the upper hand after striking a deal with Littlefinger, orders his men to take Cersei without shedding blood.

He soon realises he has been betrayed by Littlefinger.

The episode also sees the Lannisters preparing their battle and Jorah Mormont stopping an assassination attempt on Daenerys, inspiring Khal Drogo to give his blessing to lead an army against the Seven Kingdoms. Tywin is to unleash his army of 60,000 men to punish the Starks for the capture of his son Tyrion.

TRIVIA

Charles Dance makes his appearance in this episode. He said about his character Tywin, 'I think he's prepared to not necessarily forgive, but tolerate almost anything of his gorgeous, handsome son's life, because he [Jaime] is the apple of his eye. He's the epitome of perfection: tall, good-looking, great warrior, and all the rest of it. Unfortunately, his other son [Tyrion] he probably wishes he'd been smothered at birth. He's only small in stature. He has a great intellect, he has guile, he's well read – he's the only one who ever reads a book – and he's an extraordinary character. By this stage now, Tywin Lannister is having to accept that Tyrion is only small in stature. Reluctantly having to accept that he's not the awful thing he thought he was.'

Charles Dance said about Peter Dinklage, 'We're very lucky to have Peter Dinklage playing him, because he's extraordinarily gifted. He's such a great guy to work with. I have this wonderful memory of him in this film *The Station Agent*. He's a phenomenal actor, he really is [...] Now imagine if you're that size, in a world that's this size, and you have to fight even harder. And he has this wonderful talent he brings to the fore. Very bright guy, and a sweetheart, really a delightful guy. We're really lucky in that regard.'

Nikolaj Coster-Waldau, who plays Jaime, said about the scene between himself and Charles Dance, 'I was thrilled when I read the scene between Tywin and Jaime because Tywin is such an important figure in Jaime's life. He is probably the only man Jaime fears but also a man that he has immense respect for and like most sons he wants his father's approval and respect. As the readers of *A Song of Ice and Fire* know, it's a very layered relationship they have, and I thought it was great to just get the first hints of that in season one. Also because we see the relationship with Tywin's other son, Tyrion.'

While Tyrion is mentioned, he doesn't feature in the episode – the only time this happens.

Stannis is mentioned once again in this episode, but we do not meet his character until season two.

POST-ANALYSIS

Over 2.4 million viewers watched this episode in the States, stabilising the audience following the previous episode's slight slump.

Time reviewer James Poniewozik called 'You Win or You Die' the 'most thrilling and thematically rich hour to date', while *hitfix.com* said, 'What a terrific episode (probably my favourite so far), and especially in the way it turned the spotlight on the characters who are villains in Ned Stark's version of the story.'

IGN noted rather succinctly, 'S★★★ just got real.'

THE POINTY END
Season one, episode eight
Written by George R. R. Martin
Directed by Daniel Minahan

This is where it all gets interesting.

Lannister guardsmen rush at those serving the Starks in the Red Keep, killing them savagely.

A lesson between Syrio Forel and Arya is disrupted by the behemoth Ser Meryn Trant and other guardsmen, who take down several men with ease. Forel orders Arya to leave as he faces Trant with his practice sword broken and the viewer is left to presume Syrio will be defeated. Arya runs, finds her sword 'Needle' and tries to escape, accidentally piercing a stable boy who tried to capture her with the blade.

Ned has been captured, locked in the dungeons with only a passing Varys as company. The Eunuch claims he means well, but Lord Eddard Stark is wary, unsure of trusting anyone after Littlefinger's betrayal.

The manipulation continues up in the Keep, with Cersei

twisting words like a feather in the wind to ensure Sansa writes to her mother and big brother, Robb, telling them about their father's treason – a plan that is easily seen through by Robb and her mother.

Jon Snow attacks Alliser Thorne after he is taunted by him following the news that Ned Stark is a traitor, and he is confined to his quarters.

The men of Castle Black have further problems when it's discovered several men from Benjen Stark's patrol have been discovered dead. At night, one of the dead bodies comes alive and attacks the Lord Commander, played by James Cosmo. Robb tackles the mysterious being, but it doesn't die until he burns it alive. Night's Watchman Samwell Tarly tells his disbelieving friends that he read in a book that these things are brought to life by the White Walkers.

We finally see a reunion between Tywin and his son Tyrion, and as usual it is a terse one. The Imp has brought with him Bronn and members of the hill tribes. The savage warriors had tried to kill them, until Tyrion reacted with fast-talking, once again, to convince them to lead him to his father. In return, he says he will reward them with weapons so they can attack the Vale and its rulers and claim the land for themselves.

First, Tywin insists they must fight for him and, much to Tyrion's shock, he agrees to their condition that his son must fight alongside them to ensure they don't renege on the deal later. The shock to Tyrion is worsened when Tywin has them leading the attack, putting him in near certainty of death.

Elsewhere, a Dothraki raid on a village is stopped after Daenerys, outraged at their savage attacks, orders that they stop raping a woman. When Mago, one of the Dothrakis, speaks of his outrage to Khal, the warrior is tickled at Daenerys' rising power and authority – noting that it is her unborn son already showing his strength.

Mago challenges him to a fight, and it's one that Drogo dismissively agrees to, taunting him, until he finally deals the killer blow, ripping out Mago's tongue with his hands.

Drogo is wounded slightly, but dismisses it as a scratch. Daenerys insists, however, that the healer she rescued help him.

After Sansa begs for her father's life at King's Landing, Joffrey agrees to spare him, as long as he acknowledges him as King.

TRIVIA

Despite Martin having written for TV for many years, this was his first screenplay in nearly 15 years. He found the job easy because he knew the characters so well. However, the struggles came from trying to adapt to new screenplay software.

There is a slight change in Syrio Forel and the guardsmen. In the books, he is believed to have killed several of them by striking at their eyes and bones. However, the show changed the armour described in the books, making such attacks impossible. So, in the series, he just wounds them.

Martin kept the scene from the book where Arya is asked by the stable boy to take out the sword from him in his screenplay, and is unsure why it wasn't used in the episode.

Martin was often criticised by his TV bosses for making scripts that were impossible to film because of expense, and that was something that was retained for his own show. He had wanted a montage of the Northern bannermen receiving the raven from Robb who told them that a war was coming. One of those scenes was to feature Roose Bolton in the middle of flaying a man. The lengthy montage scene was dropped, with Martin noting that it would probably have cost most of the season's budget.

Martin talks of the differences between books and TV shows, giving the example of Mago, who is alive in the books but dead in the TV series.

Jason Momoa, who plays Khal Drogo, said to *Den of Geek* about his action scene, 'I shot the pilot for this, went away and did *Conan* [*the Barbarian*] and came back and shot the whole series. There was like one major scene we put into it that isn't in the book. I went up to David Benioff, and said, "I'm Conan. I've just done 17 goddamn battles. You should probably have something that shows he's this amazing warlord. He should have a little bit of a fight." I watch action movies, and you don't remember when Jason Statham does a kick or punch. It's character trait stuff you remember. Say, for instance, Indiana Jones, the guy with the sword. Indiana Jones shoots him; you remember that in the movie. The Joker in *The Dark Knight*, where he says, "Do you want to see a magic trick?" You remember that.

'It's certain punches you remember. I wanted to do something like that with Drogo. He never uses a weapon, he really gets in close. He's such a badass. It's like coming up against a silver-back bear. You don't look him in the eye. I wanted him to be that intimidating. I want to have that sense of, like, "Oh man, I'm fucked."'

Momoa continued to explain his thoughts behind playing Drogo: 'I had this dream where I wanted to rip this guy's tongue through his throat, and I thought that would be awesome. So, I had my dream come true. We did it. I said, "We don't have to make a tongue. I can just hold a chicken breast covered in blood or something like that."'

And the actor was delighted that they took his advice on board. 'They made a full throat with a tongue. So, I'm fighting this guy and he's bobbing and weaving, and I'm talking in my Dothraki tongue, and he's like, "You gotta kill me first," and I'm like, "I already have." They made that come true for me. It was great to be part of all those great artists and writers. You could be free to create the character you wanted.'

The scene where Tywin, played by Charles Dance, moves the wine cup away from Tyrion was seemingly an improvisation by the actor.

This episode was dedicated to Ralph Vicinanza – the literary agent who handled Martin's foreign language rights, and who recommended the books to Benioff and Weiss and led the negotiations with HBO. He died in his sleep from a cerebral aneurysm days after HBO green-lighted the series.

POST-ANALYSIS

The episode premiered and was seen by nearly three million viewers – a season high.

Michele Clapton, costume designer, and costume supervisor Rachael Webb-Crozier were nominated for an Emmy award for Outstanding Costumes for a Series 2011 for 'The Pointy End' but lost out to *The Borgias*.

BAELOR

Season one, episode nine
Written by David Benioff and D. B. Weiss
Directed by Alan Taylor

Aired on 12 June 2011, 'Baelor' was the episode that shocked viewers new to the series – thanks to the death of Lord Eddard Stark.

The viewer is led to believe Ned has escaped his fate after Varys visits him, once again, and begs him to pledge his allegiance to the King and Cersei, who will let him see out the rest of his life as a member of the Night's Watch if he pledges his allegiance. However, Ned declines such demands, but Varys makes one last attempt by telling him to think of his children, which seems to hit a chord with him.

Meanwhile, Daenerys has problems of her own – her beloved Drogo is struggling with the infected wound that he received from one of his own fighters. The slave healer is ordered by Daenerys to save Drogo's life, even if it's by using black magic.

Elsewhere, Robb outwits the Lannister army, capturing Jaime in the process and taking him as a prisoner.

Back in King's Landing, Stark is taken to the court, where he spots his daughter near the statue of the Great Sept of Baelor. He shouts the name Baelor to Night's

Watchman Yoren, signalling where his daughter is. Ned confesses his supposed crime, but Joffrey goes against his mother's wishes and orders him to be beheaded.

TRIVIA

'It comes as a shock to everybody – everybody, except this young little brat that's sat on the throne,' Sean Bean told *AccessHollywood.com* about his death. 'I thought it was a very dramatic ending, a very dramatic thing to do, to kill. I suppose I was playing the lead, you know, and you just get killed.

'You can play it for the kind of sympathy vote, but then you're signalling that there's gonna be some head chopping off, so I kind of, as Ned, thought, "Well, look, I've had to form an alliance with someone in order to save my children's lives." It was a wonderful moment to have the stage to yourself, as it were, and to make a speech like that. I know it's kind of tragic circumstances, but it's very enthralling, very thrilling to be acting that kind of thing.'

The drinking game between Tyrion, Bronn and Shae (Tyrion's whore) was added to the series' plot and isn't in the book.

Martin said about German actress Sibel Kekilli, who plays prostitute Shae, 'A lot of beautiful young women read for

Shae. But there's another dimension to Shae as well. She's not as practised and hardened at this as a more seasoned pro. There's still a girl-next-door quality to her, a sense of vulnerability, playfulness and, yes, innocence. All of our Shaes were hot as hell. But only a handful of them captured that other quality, maybe three out of 20, and Sibel was the standout. Watching those auditions, any red-blooded male would want to take every one of our Shae candidates to bed, but Sibel made you fall in love with her as well.'

POST-ANALYSIS

'Baelor' had 2.7 million viewers, almost matching the previous week's season high. A critic on sci-fi, fantasy blog *Suvudu* said, 'It's without a doubt my favourite episode of the season so far. Everything came together in a glorious hour of television: great writing, exceptional acting, a score that suddenly came alive in a way it hadn't before, the consummate direction of one of television's best directors.'

FIRE AND BLOOD

Season one, episode ten
Written by David Benioff and D. B. Weiss
Directed by Alan Taylor

This is the final episode of series one, which moves

swiftly, giving fans no chance to recover from the death of Ned Stark.

Ned's daughter Arya is dragged off by Yoren, who cuts off her hair so she can be passed off as a boy and go unnoticed by the Lannisters. Catelyn and Robb meet up in grief over his death, and vow to exact their revenge on the Lannisters.

King Joffrey continues to show off his violent streak, ordering a singer who penned an offensive song about his family to have his tongue ripped out. He then gleefully shows Sansa her father's decapitated head.

Tywin Lannister begrudgingly credits Tyrion for his strategic skills, and orders him to be the acting Hand to King Joffrey while he is away.

Daenerys is told by Jorah Mormont that her son has died during childbirth, and that her beloved Drogo is in a catatonic state. She kills Drogo out of mercy and constructs a pyre to burn him. She steps into the fire with the dragon eggs and miraculously survives, with the dragons hatched.

TRIVIA

Ned's head was shown early on to prove to viewers that he was dead.

'There was a bunch of viewers who had a denial reaction – that Ned couldn't possibly be dead,' said Weiss. 'However, in episode 10 we make it clear he's dead. There was a lot of discussion over how many frames of sword-into-neck to include.'

Sean Bean, who played Ned, said that, when he read Martin's book, Ned Stark's death was as much of a shock to him as anyone. 'It's a dummy of my head,' Bean said in an interview with *New York Magazine*. 'I was holding it at one point, which was a really creepy feeling, to hold my head and look at it. It was very heavy, just like a proper head!'

The show landed in hot water after Benioff and Weiss admitted that one of the heads next to Stark's was a prosthetic one of George W. Bush. They insisted it was 'not a choice, it's not a political statement. We just had to use whatever head we had around.'

The comments caused an outcry, and they tried to defuse the situation, saying, 'We use a lot of prosthetic body parts on the show: heads, arms, etc. We can't afford to have these all made from scratch, especially in scenes where we need a lot of them, so we rent them in bulk.' They added, 'After the scene was already shot, someone pointed out that one of the heads looked like George W Bush. In the DVD commentary, we mentioned this, though we should not have. We meant no disrespect to the former President and apologise if anything we said or did suggested otherwise.'

HBO was seemingly furious, and released this statement: 'We were deeply dismayed to see this and find it unacceptable, disrespectful and in very bad taste. We made this clear to the executive producers of the series who apologised immediately for this inadvertent careless mistake.

'We are sorry this happened and will have it removed from any future DVD production.'

In the commentary, Benioff and Weiss revealed that they looked at more than 200 actresses for the part of Arya. In another interview, they said, 'We are so used to seeing child roles, in television shows or movies, and in stories like this, being peripheral, and they don't have to say much. If they're doing much, it's really just acting as little innocent creatures. The kids in George's books are very, very different. Those three Stark children have amazingly important roles, and they each go off in their different directions. For the most part, they're without their parents around. They're following their own storylines. So, it was amazingly important to find the right kids, and we were terrified. Especially in Hollywood, you see so many kids, and they're adorable and very poised, and they have got mannerisms already worked out, but there is nothing very real-seeming about them. We wanted kids who were going to feel like real kids, and who had to perform in amazingly difficult scenes, watching horrible things happen to family members and just be tortured. And, those three kids delivered, beyond our imagination.'

Marillion, the singer, is maimed in the third book, but they decided to push it forward to this episode to showcase Joffrey's evil side.

One of the big scenes in the final episode is when Yoren chops off Arya's hair. The young actress who plays Arya, Maisie Williams, wore a wig for the scene, which she had to endure for five or six takes, with the production team sewing the hair pieces on, only for them to be hacked off again. It was made out of synthetic hair so it could break more easily. In season two, Williams cut her hair for real.

POST-ANALYSIS

Over three million viewers watched the episode and it was the most-watched episode of the season. The reviews were universally positive, especially for the final scene featuring Daenerys. It promised fans that they were in for a treat for the second season. *IGN* said, 'Of course, if anyone can think of a more jaw-dropping way to end things than a hot naked chick covered in smouldering ash, with three newborn dragons climbing on her, then I'll eat my iron helm.'

THE NORTH REMEMBERS
Season two, episode one
Written by David Benioff and D. B. Weiss
Directed by Alan Taylor

On 1 April 2012, the first episode of the second series began, with fans engrossed in the TV as war gripped the Seven Kingdoms.

It's King Joffrey's Name Day, and a tournament is held to celebrate the occasion. Sansa is by his side, putting on a defiant façade as a meek woman.

Tyrion makes his presence known, notifying his nephew that he will be his Hand – something that Cersei is less than happy about. Tyrion hides his lover, Shae, from everyone in the Keep after his father forbids him from seeing whores.

The viewer is finally introduced to Stannis Baratheon and his controversial adviser Melisandre – a fire sorceress. He believes he is the rightful heir to the throne, and is getting ready for the invasion of King's Landing. There is also the King of the North, Robb Stark, who demands the release of his sisters for their Lannister prisoner Jaime, not realising that Arya isn't being held captive. Renly Baratheon is also staking a claim for his place on the throne.

Rumours that Joffrey is not really Robert's son, but the

product of an incestuous affair between brother and sister, has swept through Westeros – and Joffrey gives the order to kill Robert's bastards, including, in a terrifyingly brutal scene, an infant child.

One of those bastards, Gendry, has left the city to join the Night's Watch, along with Arya, who is now posing as a boy.

As for Daenerys, her numbers have diminished following the death of Drogo and they are facing starvation, so she continues to seek shelter for her loyal people.

TRIVIA

Carice van Houten was asked to audition for another part in season one before landing the role of Melisandre, but scheduling conflicts prevented that.

Weiss admitted there were deviations from the second book, but 'only because there are characters that are off screen in the book. A lot of the changes keep people front and centre who are very important characters.' Benioff added, 'We're adapting *A Song of Ice and Fire*. So we're bringing in elements from *A Storm of Swords*. We don't think of this season as being strictly an adaptation of *A Clash of Kings*, it's really a continuation of our adaptation of the series as a whole. For our purposes, moving some stuff forward helps a lot and pushing some stuff back helps us a lot.'

The budget was extended for season two. Benioff told *Entertainment Weekly*, 'This season is about a country at war. And we felt like, if we didn't see the most important battle of this entire war onscreen, we're going to short-change viewers.'

Weiss added, 'To my knowledge, a story of this scale has never been told within filmed entertainment. There's so many characters and locations and storylines, so many things that are atypical in television, and for good reason. You could do this show relatively easily, with twice the money that we have, then after a couple great seasons it'd collapse under its own weight and cease to exist. We went in asking for more money, a considerable sum, in order to shoot the battle scenes. We didn't get everything we wanted. But it [the conversation with HBO] wasn't about "Will this attract more viewers? Is this something that's gonna pump ratings?" It was all about why this story needs this big battle. And so it was really a long conversation about how the second season builds towards it [a battle sequence].'

POST-ANALYSIS

Unsurprisingly, with it being the debut episode of the second season, the ratings were its highest yet, hitting 3.8 million. The additional airings of the night saw that figure nearly double.

THE NIGHT LANDS

Season two, episode two
Written by David Benioff and D. B. Weiss
Directed by Alan Taylor

Aired on 8 April 2012, 'The Night Lands' saw the series back to its political plotting best, with the episode showing the different rulers making their plans to either invade King's Landing or protect it. Ser Davos, the right-hand man of Stannis, seeks out help to bolster their army, with Robb Stark sending Theon to the Iron Islands where he grew up in a bid to win an alliance – while Cersei and Tyrion try to mend their differences for the sake of the throne.

Tyrion's attempts to keep Shae secret from the people of the Red Keep doesn't last long, and it should be no surprise that it's Varys who does the discovering. But, with Varys back-slapping himself with the notion that he has the upper hand against Tyrion, the acting Hand begins to show that he has his own skills of deceit and manipulation.

Theon's belief that he will be welcomed with joyous celebration by his father is misplaced. Theon was placed in the care of Ned Stark after his father and his people attempted, and failed, to rebel against Robert – and by taking his only living male heir it ensured he wouldn't do anything like that again. Ned raised the boy well and looked after him, and Theon's inner battle about where his loyalty lies is something that begins to torment him.

Jon Snow and other Night's Watch members are holed up at Craster's farm for brief shelter during their expedition Beyond the Wall. Snow discovers that Craster keeps his daughters as wives and gives his baby sons to the White Walkers.

TRIVIA

Fantasy plays a bigger part in season two, with Weiss noting, 'We're well within the bounds of groundedness. When supernatural things happen, they happen infrequently enough that they're still startling. By the time the next thing comes along, your roots in the story are deep enough that it doesn't yank you out.'

Liam Cunningham, who plays Davos, didn't feature in season one but studied it. 'It was a no brainer,' he told *SFX*. 'When I got the 10 DVDs, I said I'll watch two a day for five days, and of course as anybody who knows the show knows, as soon as you put the first one in, well... I managed to get through six the first time, and went to bed about five in the morning, and as soon as I got up, I watched the other four. So I watched them all over about a 14-hour period. It wasn't difficult, it's beautifully crafted television. It is intelligent, thought provoking, in your face, joy to watch and certainly a joy to be a part of.'

Explaining his thoughts on knowing the fate of his character, Cunningham explained to *SFX*, 'I'm no fool. I want to know that I'm not going to get killed in episode two and stuff like that, but I don't really want to pursue his journey so much through the books. He's a great character, and I'm enjoying what he does. Sometimes, naivety is a good thing. Davos is a point-of-view character, so unless I'm standing there brooding with a narration in the background, which would reflect the book, then they have to formulate this guy where he's in the scene and interacting with these other characters. So that's a fresh view, in a sense, of the character. I'm acting the script, not the books. I'm eagerly awaiting reading them when I'm finally laid to rest, whenever that may be.'

Working on season two, did Emilia Clarke miss working with Harry Lloyd and Jason Momoa, who played Viserys and Khal respectively? 'Yeah, hugely,' she said. 'Harry came to the screenings of episodes one and two of season two the other night, and I hang out with Jason all the time. It's very sad being on set without them, but in that sense it fuels the character because it's sad for the character as well. Everything you feel as an actor, you can put into your work so in that sense it was helpful, but at the same time it was a quieter set.'

Gemma Whelan, who plays Theon's warrior sister, said about her audition, 'I had been to a different audition, but I was told I would be good for this other thing called *Game of Thrones*. So I said, "That sounds interesting," but I didn't know anything about it. And then I went the following week to my first audition, but I had watched a bit of it, and seen little bits of Alfie [Allen, who plays Theon] and whatnot. But I didn't know what I was getting myself into until I went to my first audition and could see just how exciting this could be. I had to pretend I was pleasuring a man on a chair.'

POST-ANALYSIS

Game of Thrones was still attracting big numbers, pulling in 3.8 million. The success certainly pleased HBO bosses – who renewed the show for a third season shortly after the second episode debuted.

The controversy about the show's sexual content would rear its head again, with many critics asking whether the amount of nudity was really needed. *SFX* wrote, 'This week, we're treated to the seedy reality behind the scenes at a King's Landing brothel and a brother and sister horse ride that is several different shades of wrong. It'd be enough to make you sick in your mouth if it wasn't so bloody entertaining, and true to form *Game of Thrones* continues to intrigue and titillate in equal measure.'

WHAT IS DEAD MAY NEVER DIE
Season two, episode three
Written by Bryan Cogman
Directed by Alik Sakharov

Jon Snow is rebuked by Lord Commander Jeor Mormont after he is caught spying on Craster. When Jon tells him that Craster is giving his young sons as sacrifices to the White Walkers, Mormont admits that he has known all along.

Renly's worries about consummating his marriage to Queen Margaery go unfounded, after she tells him that she knows that he's in love with her brother, and she doesn't care. She just wants to be Queen and produce an heir, and doesn't care that he is gay.

Theon continues to be mocked by his father and sister Yara. He is stunned when he is told he can take a sole ship for small raids, while his sister is put in command of thirty boats.

Summoning up newfound courage, Theon blasts back at his father for abandoning him, but by the end he has sworn his allegiance to his family, burning a note that he had originally planned to send to Robb warning him of his father's plans.

Tyrion shows that he has what it takes to survive among the high powers at King's Landing, with some canny manipulation of his own, telling Pycelle, Littlefinger and Varys conflicting stories in the hope that one of the stories will work its way into Cersei's ear. It turns out Pycelle is the mole, and Tyrion has Bronn arrest him.

Yoren is killed by Lannister's soldiers for not giving up Gendry as he takes the group of men (and Arya) to the Night's Watch. Arya tricks them into thinking that they've killed Gendry, but they are all captured and taken to a nearby castle.

TRIVIA

The episode's title comes from an Iron Islands phrase.

Renly and Loras were never actually confirmed as being lovers in the book, with Martin only implying that the two men were boyfriends. However, he has since confirmed in the TV series that they were in fact in a relationship.

Story editor Bryan Cogman revealed how Ros, who is not mentioned in the books, came to be a part of the *Game of Thrones* world.

He said, 'That's a David and Dan special. She doesn't even exist in the books. Ros was originally "Red Headed Whore Number 1" in the pilot. In the very original [draft], Tyrion was in a brothel in King's Landing as a way to introduce him and get a little download of information about Jon Arryn. For various budgetary reasons in the pilot, we couldn't shoot King's Landing at all or have any King's Landing sets, so what you ended up seeing is where Tyrion has skipped out on the royal procession and tries to find Winterfell's brothel... Ros the whore kind of emerged from that.

'With season two, there's a character in the book named Alayaya, who we didn't end up keeping. We knew that Ros would serve that function in the latter part of the season, where Cersei thinks she's caught Tyrion's girlfriend but actually has caught Ros and doesn't know who she is. We had that in place, it's funny, it's one of those things that kind of happened by accident. You're finding different ways as you're plotting the season to examine different traits and characters.

'There's a throwaway line in the second book where Tyrion says, "Oh, we should hire some whores for Joffrey, maybe that would let him calm down a bit", and we thought, we have to see that scene. What ended up emerging was that horrific – as horrific as anything in the show – scene where Ros and Daisy are made to abuse each other for Joffrey's sick jollies. And then, the other thing that we sort of built into the show was the rivalry between Littlefinger and Varys. Ros seemed to be the perfect person for Varys to have an insider in Littlefinger's company; she came to Littlefinger, trusted him, thought she had a rapport, and sort of had a rude awakening about who she is, and who she is in Littlefinger's eyes.'

POST-ANALYSIS

The episode matched the previous week's figures of 3.8 million viewers, cementing its status as one of television's biggest shows. *Hitfix.com* reviewed the episode: 'This is a season of many kings, and many gods, all in a struggle for supremacy, and with it a lot of debate over what truly defines power. As a non-reader of the books, I have no idea where this is all going, but I have a feeling we're going to get evidence of what kind of power truly reigns supreme in Westeros. And in "What Is Dead May Never Die" we get practical demonstrations of many different kinds.'

GARDEN OF BONES

Season two, episode four
Written by Vanessa Taylor
Directed by David Petrarca

With so much infighting and back-stabbing, *Game of Thrones* makes an attempt at peace and friendship in this episode. Of course, these attempts ultimately fail.

Catelyn hopes to persuade warring brothers Renly and

Stannis to come to a truce and fight the Lannisters together, but they both refuse, and vow to battle each other for their right to overthrow the King.

Daenerys attempts to find shelter for her people and leads them to the extravagant and luxurious city of Qarth. Behind its lavishly clothed leaders and glorious architecture lies danger, as the city is famed for its Warlocks who reside there. But she's desperate and pleads to be let in.

Tyrion, fearing that his cruel nephew is getting worse after he is forced to stop him attacking Sansa, decides to surprise him with two prostitutes. However, Joffrey shows his sadistic streak by making one of the girls, Ros, viciously beat up the other one.

Arya and Gendry are taken to Harrenhal, where they are imprisoned and wait their turn to be tortured by having a rat burrow through their chests, as punishment and as a way of extracting answers from them. However, Tywin comes just as it's Gendry's turn and rebukes his men for wasting lives, when they could be put to better use. He also quickly points out that Arya is a girl posing as a boy, but he doesn't recognise her as a Stark. When she is asked why, she tells him it's less dangerous if you look like a boy while travelling the roads.

Tywin is impressed with her smartness and makes her his new cupbearer. What Tywin doesn't know is that Arya now has unique access to Tywin's plans on and off the battlefield.

It also allows the viewer a sneak peek into Tywin's world, through the eyes of someone else.

The episode ends with Melisandre and Davos rowing into some caves located near Renly's camp, all on Stannis' command. It is here that Melisandre reveals that she is heavily pregnant and promptly gives birth to a creature made entirely of shadow, as Davos looks on in horror

TRIVIA

Author Martin himself has said about the series, 'I like the fact that David [Benioff] and Dan [Weiss] are doing a faithful adaptation so, when the scenes are the scenes from the books, I like those. And I like almost all of the new scenes, not from the books, that David and Dan and the other writers have added. The only thing that I miss is the scenes that are left out, scenes from the books that are not included in the TV show that I wish they would have included.

The Joffrey scene led to a huge Twitter debate about whether Ros was forced to sodomise Daisy with a stag's head sceptre or beat her up with it.

Esmé Bianco, who plays Ros, quickly clarified to the *Daily Beast*, 'What got cut from the edit was that I was beating her and you see the sceptre coming down [with] blood on the end of it … I'm [actually] hitting a pillow. I had to hit it with all my force, and I broke the sceptre. People were gluing it back together because antlers were coming off.

'No matter where any of the characters think they've gotten to in terms of power, there's always somebody that's willing to beat them down. It's the one time that we see Ros where her sex appeal does nothing for her and doesn't get her out of that situation. It's not about her being a prostitute; it's about her being just another person that Joffrey is going to stomp on.'

POST-ANALYSIS

The ratings dipped slightly but it was still a well-reviewed episode. However, the *Guardian* had an issue with the violence, saying, 'This was an exceptionally violent episode. It featured: one death by a Direwolf; one graphic foot amputation; two separate uses of a crossbow as a weapon of intimidation; the continued humiliation of Sansa, stripped and beaten on Joffrey's orders; the brutal whipping of a whore, again, at Joffrey's command; two torture scenes (one of which was interrupted); a couple of backhanders; several dead bodies and one (slightly camp) Qartheen blood oath.'

THE GHOST OF HARRENHAL
Season two, episode five
Written by David Benioff and D. B. Weiss
Directed by David Petrarca

Episode two ended with Davos taking Melisandre onshore on a secret mission, which saw her bringing a shadow monster into the world.

The start of this episode sees it promptly kill Renly. His new Kingsguard, Brienne, is falsely accused of the crime, and she flees with Catelyn, who happens to see Renly die at the hands of the dark magic, too.

Tyrion, in this episode, continues with his cunning ploys to keep ahead of his sister, and he discovers that she is squirrelling away lots of the powerful and flammable substance known as wildfire. He hatches his own plan with the deadly substance.

Theon hatches a plan to show his father that he can be a true leader by taking over his old home – Winterfell.

Arya Stark meets up with a mysterious man she saved earlier in the series. He is Jaqen H'ghar, who we later learn is a Faceless Man – one of a group of shadowy assassins. Because Arya saved his life, he grants her something in return: he will kill three people of her choosing, and, as the first name, she targets the torturer.

TRIVIA

Alfie Allen, as Theon, was the brunt of several practical jokes: 'Oh, yeah, basically this script was given to me that indicates that Bran kills me in Winterfell, and I just die. People expected me to just say, "Wait a minute, I died?" I didn't see it that way at all, actually, I thought it was great – it was really well written.

'I was on holiday in Ibiza, actually, and David and Dan called me after and asked how I felt about it. And I was, "Yeah, yeah, that's cool." And I think they were hoping I'd give them more of a reaction, so then they say, "We've had this other idea. We want you to be a zombie for the next series. Is that cool? We'd like you to be a zombie with no dialogue whatsoever." And I said, "Okay, uh, all right, if that's what you want, guys, let's do it, let's go for it." Because I feel so happy and lucky to be on this amazing show, I'm not going to throw a fit or put my foot down, you know? Obviously if I think something isn't right for the character, I'd speak up. But they're just so on the ball and amazing writers, that everything they write [even the prank script] was so perfect.'

POST-ANALYSIS

HBO bosses were left celebrating after the show gained its best ratings to date – getting over 3.9 million viewers. It had been something of a slow burner, like HBO had predicted – correctly guessing that it would attract an audience through word of mouth.

The *Telegraph's* review called it 'a classic mid-series episode. Aside from Renly's brisk death, most of the action was expository rather than climactic.'

THE OLD GODS AND THE NEW

Season two, episode six
Written by Vanessa Taylor
Directed by David Nutter

This gripping episode certainly starts off with a bang: Theon Greyjoy has taken over Winterfell, and Maester Luwin – who is a caring figure for the Stark boys and a loyal member of the Starks and Winterfell – desperately sends off a raven messenger to warn Jon Snow about his former friend. Young Bran and Luwin beg Theon to reconsider, and Theon promises no one will die if Bran surrenders. He does so, but Rodrik Cassel spits in Theon's face, and ironborn raider Dagmer Cleftjaw insists Theon must kill Rodrik if he wants to be respected by his men. Reluctantly, Theon beheads him, much to Bran's shock.

The wildling Osha, who now looks after Bran like a nanny, hatches a plan for her, Bran, Rickon Stark and Hodor to escape, but first she must seduce Theon. She has sex with him, but, when he is sleeping, she sneaks out – taking Bran, Rickon and Hodor with her.

At the army camp in the Westerlands, Catelyn Stark meets up with her son Robb, and he introduces her to a nurse called Talisa. She senses their attraction, but later reminds Robb of his obligations and that he is already betrothed to Lord Frey's daughter (see entry entitled 'Red Wedding' for further information). They are told by Roose Bolton that Winterfell has been taken by Theon and his men.

Robb reluctantly agrees to not withdraw his huge army of troops to rescue his brothers, and allows a small Northern group to take back Winterfell.

At King's Landing, Joffrey's reign is bringing dissent from the people and he is pelted with excrement by rioting peasants when he leaves the castle walls. Joffrey demands they are executed, but a riot breaks out and, among other acts of riotous behaviour, Sansa is nearly raped by the mob, until the Hound saves her.

Daenerys attempts to find resources to buy ships are fruitless, and she returns to her room to finds her dragons missing and members of her entourage killed, including Irri.

TRIVIA

Dothraki Irri, a recurring character in series one and two, does not die in the books, but had to be killed off as the actress Amrita Acharia couldn't secure her EU work visa.

In the book, she is in a sex scene with Daenerys, which will now obviously never be shown. There was a proper death scene filmed, but it was never aired. She explained, 'I'm waiting for Daenerys to come back so I'm running up the stairs. "Khaleesi, are you back yet?" And the dragons are gone. Out of nowhere, there's a noose around my neck. I think it's hard to be strangled on screen because obviously to an extent, to make it look real, you really have to be a bit strangled. So I had massive bruises on my neck the next day; I was proud. Battle scars. Death scenes are fun.'

POST-ANALYSIS

The reviewers were ecstatic with the episode, with many calling it the best of the series so far, and the ratings were roughly the same as the week before.

Neela Debnath writing for the *Independent* wrote, 'The pace may be slow but when the rewards come they are big and this week was a fantastic episode that was well worth the wait... Once again, this episode has surpassed the one before it.'

A MAN WITHOUT HONOR

Season two, episode seven
Written by David Benioff and D. B. Weiss
Directed by David Nutter

After learning that Osha has escaped with the two Starks and Hodor, Theon hunts them down to a farm, but he has been tricked into believing they are there. Bran cleverly uses his wolf's scent to trick them. Theon supposedly kills the two children he has found living there, burns them and then passes the charred bodies off as Bran and Rickon Stark.

To her horror, Sansa finds her sheets covered in blood, and she realises she has begun menstruating – and can now have Joffrey's child. She desperately tries to hide the evidence, but the Hound finds out and all is revealed to Cersei. This leads to a slightly warm – if bizarre, given the circumstance – meeting with Cersei, who recounts her births.

Cersei also shares a moment with Tyrion, with the pair taking a break from needling each other with vicious asides and hurtful acts. She confesses that she believes her son is the product of her and Jaime's sinful act. Tyrion comforts her, by telling her that her two other children are good people.

Jaime is sharing a cage with his cousin, but he kills him in a bid to escape. However, he is recaptured, and it soon becomes clear to Catelyn that the soldiers are desperate to kill him – robbing her of the chance to use him as an exchange for her daughter.

After Jon is left alone by his scouting group to execute a

female wilding, his reluctance allows her to escape. She is recaptured by Jon, but he has lost his group. She taunts him about the way he lives his life – taking orders and swearing an oath that he could never be with a girl. When she escapes again, he blindly follows her – not realising he is being led into an ambush.

TRIVIA

The scene where Jaime Lannister is surrounded by an angry baying mob desperate for his blood was based loosely on the footage of Libyan dictator Muammar Gaddafi's death, which had just been broadcast on the news. Director David Nutter wanted to catch the energy of pure bloodthirsty vengeance.

The title comes from a line uttered with contempt by Catelyn to Jaime Lannister.

It's the first time the phrase 'War of the Five Kings' is said on screen. It is said by actor Charles Dance, who plays Tywin Lannister.

The scene where Jaime Lannister kills his cousin in a bid to facilitate his escape was hailed by actor Nikolaj Coster-Waldau as his best working experience.

POST-ANALYSIS

The *Telegraph* gave it five stars, noting, 'Perhaps what makes so many people susceptible to *Game of Thrones*: all of the characters, even the incestuous child-killers, are somehow loveable.'

Den of Geek reviewed the episode and said, 'This week, penned by David Benioff and D. B. Weiss, was beautifully sharp on the dialogue front... *Thrones* and its creative crew have been working very hard not to make any character one-note.'

THE PRINCE OF WINTERFELL

Season two, episode eight
Written by David Benioff and D. B. Weiss
Directed by Alan Taylor

Aired on 20 May 2012, the episode was geared towards the Battle of the Blackwater. Stannis is close to his destination King's Landing (thanks to a big fleet led in part by Davos), and Tyrion tries desperately to ensure his risky plan of using the flammable potion wildfire will work to fend off the invaders.

Jon Snow plans to infiltrate the wildings army by posing as one of them after he is captured by the Lord of Bones, a member of the wildings.

Robb Stark is furious when he learns that his mother has Jaime, sending him along under the watchful eye of Brienne to ensure he is exchanged for her daughters. He orders his mother to be kept under guard, and Robb ends up in the arms of Talisa – defying his betrothal to House Frey.

TRIVIA

An ever-present director on *Game of Thrones*, Alan Taylor won't be around for series three as he will be directing *Thor 2*.

To better portray the land Beyond the Wall, Benioff and Weiss chose Iceland over filming in a studio with a green-screen backdrop. Weiss said, 'Our general approach with everything is, if there's something real that we can build on and use effects to turn into our world, that's always better. It's always going to be better to start with a real foundation, whether it's a castle or a canyon encampment, or whatever. In Iceland, there's not a damn thing you need to do. It looks like no other place on earth.'

Not that it didn't pose its own problems. 'There was a shot where Samwell's talking to Jon and he looks normal,' said Benioff. 'You cut to Jon, then you cut back to Samwell and he looks like Father Time – like with the snow and the ice just frozen onto his face in just a matter of seconds. It's really hard to do continuity. But they [the actors] never complained once.'

Weiss added, 'I knew it was gonna be pretty rough [on Kit Harington] and there's no shelter out there for six, eight hours in very cold conditions. And I went up to talk to Kit on his first day of shooting and asked, "How you doing?" He said, "I've never ever had a day of shooting that I loved as much as this."'

A costume designer can only submit one episode for Emmy consideration, and Michele Clapton chose this one. She had originally wanted to showcase the more flamboyant and glamorous side of the show, but she instead thought, 'Don't take that route, be braver,' and chose this episode to show how the costumes could be different in this kind of genre. Out went the original plan to show royal gowns and in came the Inuit-inspired costumes of the wildings, with animal skins, and leather and animal bones lashed together to serve as battle armour. 'We bought a lot of bones online from eBay,' she told the *Hollywood Reporter*. 'Then we took moulds of the bones and made armour, all strapped together with what looks like guts but is actually string and latex.'

POST-ANALYSIS

Impressively the show's ratings refused to drop, with critics mainly enjoying the episode. However, most critics noted that it was essentially a nice lull before the next episode's major battle.

Tom Chivers, for the *Telegraph*, wrote, 'Loyalty and betrayal, oath-breaking and oath-keeping. They're always themes in *Game of Thrones*, but this week they came to the fore. Almost every character had a decision to make: who to be loyal to, when it meant betraying someone else.'

BLACKWATER

Season two, episode nine
Written by George R. R. Martin
Directed by Neil Marshall

With a screenplay by Martin and direction by acclaimed Scottish filmmaker Neil Marshall, there was an impressive pedigree to oversee the iconic Battle of Blackwater. Unsurprisingly, a large portion of the strategic warfare and epic moments in Martin's book were either toned down or excised completely. Unbelievably, however, HBO was at one time considering having the battle take place off screen in a bid to rein in the budget.

Benioff and Weiss argued their case persuasively; thankfully, because this was the biggest, and most expensive, moment to hit the series: huge explosions, graphic deaths, sweeping shots and flaming arrows. Yet, those aren't necessarily the parts that stay with you…

A drunken Cersei spitting out insults while holed up in the room below with the women added some humour to the proceedings, but also showed her contempt at being forced into a room of people she doesn't want to be with purely because she is a female. Tyrion desperate to find his secret love just so he can see her possibly for the last time, and Bronn and Tyrion saying good luck to each other, also provided a good aside to the battle scenes.

But the most heartbreaking moment is the realisation that it's all over, and Cersei comforts her youngest son Tommen, reaching for some poison she has acquired to kill him before the invading army arrives. She hears the footsteps, apparently of Stannis, and is inches away from giving him poison, until, at the last minute, she realises it's her father telling her the battle has been won.

Other major plot developments occur in this episode. Most noteworthy include Tyrion being left for dead after heroically taking as many men as possible into battle – despite his size – after Joffrey decides to run back into the castle to safety, showing him up to be a coward. Frightened by the wildfire and flames (fire burned his face as a boy), the Hound also deserts the battle, leaving King's Landing behind him. Nearly all of Stannis Baratheon's ships are burned away by the wildfire, leaving only a handful of ships still on the sea. Although Davos' ship goes under during the battle, he survives the fire but is left for dead.

TRIVIA

Director Neil Marshall wasn't the first choice, but the original director pulled out at the last minute. Benioff said he 'went pleading to HBO for more money [for the episode]. We made our case why we needed the battle and they obliged.'

Talking about the battle, Benioff explained, 'It was pretty much a month straight of night shoots, which is just tough for anybody unless you're a vampire. It's Belfast nights, which means it's cold and it's usually wet. There was an incredible amount of mud. It's tough for the crew, but then when you see it on screen and see how good it looks, you see the way the weather affects people. You see the wind blowing their hair and the rain coming down. None of that's faked.'

Sophie Turner said about the episode, 'She [Sansa] wants to go back to Winterfell and see her family again, but, after being caged up, she's learned not to trust anyone. She knows her family isn't going to be like it is in the fairytales, waiting for her return. She hears that her brother is fighting a war, and she knows it's never going to be the same. It's not like she has a plan to get out, because she's only thinking about her survival now, and she's kind of just going with the flow. But she's very broken, kind of stunned and traumatised, and it's hard for her to function without the people who love her. I would love to see Sansa marry for love, but, after what's happened with Joffrey, I think it'll be hard for her to trust anyone.'

POST-ANALYSIS

Critics seemed to love the episode, with many calling it the best hour of TV in that year. However, it was one of the lowest figures of the year. But it was shown around the Memorial Day holiday in US, a time that often hurts programme ratings.

IGN gave a glowing review; 'The episode "Blackwater" was nothing short of a stunning triumph. We might have had a few *Game of Thrones* episodes in the past that felt like they heavily focused on one story as an anchor, but never an episode that truly stayed *with only one* scenario the entire time. And what a freakin' fantastic journey it was.'

VALAR MORGHULIS

Season two, episode ten
Written by David Benioff and D. B. Weiss
Directed by Alan Taylor

At the end of the episode 'Blackwater', we are led to believe that Tyrion has died, but it transpires that he was saved on the battlefield. Left a wounded man with only half a face, Tyrion still hopes that he will be rewarded for his efforts. However, much to his dismay, rather than being hailed a hero for taking the men into battle, and plotting to release the wildfire to stop Stannis attacking King's Landing, a wounded Tyrion is a forgotten man, forced out of sight, with his father taking all the credit for winning the battle. The thing that keeps Tyrion's spirits up is the confirmation that Shae still wants to stay by his side, despite his disfigured face and wounded body. However, both the positivity and negativity just encourage Tyrion to build up all his strength to begin plotting again.

Joffrey rewards those who helped him in need, and agrees to wed Margaery, relieving Sansa of her duties. Thinking she is free, Littlefinger warns her that he will still have plenty of use for her.

At Winterfell, Theon is surrounded and he knows it's over. Luwin tells him to escape through the tunnels and join the Night's Watch, as, once you take your oath, your sins are forgotten. But Theon thinks it's too late, and he decides to meet the army. He performs a rousing cry to arms, but, after he's finished his speech encouraging men to follow him into battle, his own men knock him out, leaving him for dead. Luwin tries to help him, but is stabbed in the chest and later dies.

Daenerys arrives at the House of the Undying in a bid to get her dragons back. The Warlock tries to trick her into meeting Drogo in her fantasy world, but she shows her toughness by walking away from him and fights the Warlock with her dragons, burning him alive.

Jon Snow is left to defend the Wall and his brothers on the Night's Watch by pretending to be a turned cloak after being captured by the Others. This means he has to convince Mance Rayder and the Others that he is now one of them, in order to work out their future plans.

The final scene sees the White Walkers and the wights walk through the frozen landscape. Jon Snow is captured by the Others.

TRIVIA

The term Valar Morghulis is a common greeting in the Free City of Braavos, and roughly translates to 'all men must die'. A response often uttered back is Memento Mori, which means 'all men must serve'.

This episode was 10 minutes longer than the other episodes to allow time to move on from the events of the Battle of the Blackwater, while also setting up the events for the eagerly awaited third season.